Challenge of Youth

Endpaper: Members
of the Berlin
Pfadfinder group in
Grunewald, 1932.

Overleaf: A page
from Aucherbach's
Calendar of German
Youths, 1935.

Challenge of Youth

Youth

Friedrich Heer

The University of Alabama Press   *University, Alabama*

© Friedrich Heer, 1974
Translated from the German by Geoffrey Skelton
Picture research by Gun Brinson
Originally published by
George Weidenfeld and Nicolson Ltd., 1974
Published in the United States of America
by The University of Alabama Press, 1974
Library of Congress catalog card number 74-10106
ISBN 0-8173-5000-4

Contents

Introduction: What is a youth movement?   7

Restless youth up to 1770   15

Youth and the great revolution   23

The Romantic reaction   39

Boy scouts and Christian youth associations   55

The German youth movement, 1897–1933   63

Young revolutionaries in eastern Europe   76

Youth as human material   103

Youth problems since 1945   119

Youth unrest in Britain and America   133

Youth rebellion in Europe, 1960–70   164

Permanent revolution in Latin America   192

Young revolutionaries in China and Japan   197

A look at the present and future   214

Acknowledgments   219

Index   220

Introduction: What is a youth movement?

Rebellion among the young against the old is no new phenomenon, though we tend to see current manifestations of 'youth culture' or the 'youth revolution' as peculiar to our own time. The hippies, the provos and the New Left of the West today, and even the young Red Guards of communist China, have in a general sense their roots in generational conflicts that date back at least to Greek and Roman times; and in a far more specific sense the rebel German students now reading Marcuse, Reich, and Che Guevara are also the direct heirs of a long line of Lutheran non-conformists descended from Thomas Müntzer and the Peasants' Revolts of the sixteenth century.

On the other hand, for thousands of years in human history, no one felt impelled even to define 'youth' as a concept. In the closed communities of ancient times, boys were brought up to manhood and admitted to the society of adult men in ritual initiation ceremonies, of which remnants can be seen in the confirmation rites of Christian churches today. Girls were brought up by women to become the wives of men. Only when young people began to behave in a 'problematic' way, when a distinct contrast between them and their elders became apparent, did the word 'youth' come to be used generically.

And a youth movement, in the very general sense in which we shall define it for the purposes of this study, can be said to exist only when young people of an identifiable social group have felt themselves at some definite time in history to be at loggerheads, as a whole, with an older generation, and were recognised by that older generation as a counter-force to be denounced as disrespectful, rebellious and revolutionary.

In the civilisations of both Ancient Greece and

What is a youth movement?

Opposite: A group of young people at the Isle of Wight Festival, 1970.
Below: Countless bronze statues of Classical Antiquity have been preserved; they give us a good picture of the Greek ideal of youth: this Roman copy of a Greek original dates from the fourth century.

Rome there occurred periods of crisis in which groups of young people were specifically involved. These groups could indeed be regarded as early youth movements. In Greece they occurred around 400 BC and – probably – in the Hellenistic period or even before the arrival of Alexander the Great. In Rome a group centred around Scipio Aemilianus, as we know from Sallust, and another arose in the time of Cicero and Caesar.

In Attica restless youths gathered around Socrates, Alcibiades, and the Sophists: an English relief of the nineteenth century shows Socrates surrounded by his young pupils.

In the great vacuum which succeeded the collapse of all belief in the old political and religious order, the elders in Greece were perturbed to see their young people evolving a sort of counter-culture of their own, openly directed against the established customs of their parents. It rejected all existing educational patterns and social conventions. It proclaimed sexual freedom and sought new political saviours and new gods. This restless circle of young

people was centred around Socrates, Alcibiades and the Sophists.

Where Rome was concerned, Otto Seel has demonstrated that Catilina and his young companions were not simply a criminal band out to destroy the Roman republic, but the historical expression of a period of crisis in the first century BC. For centuries the Romans had accorded recognition only to the adult man – indeed only to the old man, the *senex*. It was Cicero who, in the great generation battle of his time, first discovered the intrinsic value of youth. Growing up in the shadow of Sulla's brutal dictatorship, recognising in the sacrosanct ideals of their fathers only the decorative slogans of self-interest, these young Roman city-dwellers saw themselves as a lost generation. They were filled with hatred, hope and despair, torn between rebellion and resignation.

It is the concern of this book to set modern youth rebellions in the context of the past; and to try to suggest some particular characteristics of specifically youthful revolt. These characteristics may apply to a whole movement, or they may colour a wider movement to which youth contributes. But they are the specific contribution of the young to human change through the ages.

What one might call the 'crown prince conflict' has long been familiar to us in Celtic legend and Ancient Greek drama, through Shakespeare's royal dramas and, in more recent history, in the struggle between the Austrian emperor Franz Joseph and his son Rudolf. Such individual conflicts do not of course constitute 'youth movements.' But the symbolic rejection of the father (authority), and frequent adoption of a new 'father' (today it might be Lenin or Mao Tse-tung), can be seen in more general rebellions of youth, giving them their specific emotional drive. Political revolutionary feelings often spring directly from the passions generated in the family.

A characteristic vision of liberation that goes beyond the political and economic can frequently be found in youthful rebellion. It demands liberation

of the whole personality – sexual freedom, creative freedom. It envisages a 'cultural revolution' to realise the full human potential. And simply because these drives are strongest in the young, and youth passes, youthful rebellion has a special emphemeral quality.

The deeds of Theseus pictured on this Greek bowl reflect the spirit of the youths in ancient Greece.

History has shown that youth movements flare up suddenly at the crisis points of a civilisation, and are often just as suddenly stamped out. Their leaders fall or flee, their comrades disperse. The hidden after-effects are often not seen for generations, and then not always recognised for what they are: fire from ashes. The immortality of the great youth movements of history rests on a series of short-lived dramatic events, each uncompleted, imperfect and apparently unvictorious.

The disillusioned young Greeks around Socrates, the young rebels around Catilina and the later ones at the time of Shelley, Byron, Blake, Hölderlin, are all parts of an unfinished symphony. Defeat, the death of the young hero, poet, thinker, revolutionary; *Ver Sacrum, sacre du printemps,* the sacrificial death ritualised into harmless initiation ceremonies: what does all this mean in the harsh light of historical fact but that every significant youth movement is in its own time crushed by the forces in power, and its spirit frequently perverted or bent to other uses? It is the fathers who in the end have the last word.

The Old Testament ends with the words: 'Behold, I will send you Elijah the prophet before the coming of the great and dreadful day of the Lord. And he shall turn the heart of the fathers to the children, and the heart of the children to their fathers, lest I come and smite the earth with a curse.' It is worth noting that here the precondition of saving the world from destruction, of averting the 'final solution', is that *first* the fathers shall turn to the children – in their hearts, the mainspring of all they are and all they do.

Restless youth up to 1770

Back to the origins of Western Christian civilisation, there are glimpses to be had of young people in revolt, which strike contemporary chords of sympathy. Indeed, Franz Rosenzweig, one of the greatest Jewish thinkers of our century, has described Christianity itself as a 'romantic Jewish youth movement.' Epigrammatic as the phrase may be, it reflects the special role of the young in early Christianity, and in later movements for religious reform against the established Church; and stresses the anti-authoritarian, idealist love elements in Christianity's purest forms, both characteristic of the ideology of youth.

Jesus, the young Jew, was *not* fighting against the Father God of Israel. But his struggle to revitalise Jewish piety by basing it on a direct divine relationship between father and son (a conception made possible, as David Flusser has pointed out, by the refinement of Jewish sensibilities in the century and a half before Christ's appearance) could easily have appeared to orthodox believers as the rebellion of a son against his father. All the more so, since this young citizen of a spiritually and politically disordered people openly attacked all the existing father figures. He and his 'uneducated' friends from the provinces denounced the overbearing father-priests in the train of the high priest in Jerusalem. Had not they turned God's temple into a prison and sold Israel into slavery? But it was not only this corrupt establishment of the ancient Jewish hierarchy that Jesus opposed. He was also against their protector, the Emperor in Rome, and all Romans who saw themselves as super-fathers.

Youth movement characteristics can be seen in many of the groups of idealists formed during the pre-Constantine Christian era in Asia Minor, Syria, Egypt, North Africa and Spain. Not infrequently

Opposite:
Joan of Arc, barely seventeen, routs the English at Orleans. Throughout the ages she has remained the symbol of valiant European youth.

these young communities were led by women. Their enthusiastic religious services remind us today of hippy ceremonies. (It is no accident that both hippies and yippies regard Jesus as one of themselves.) St Paul was shocked by their combinations of song and dance and 'inspired' speech. Between his time and that of St Augustine, emotional communities of this sort were either disbanded or severely disciplined by the church.

The Middle Ages

In the early years of Christianity orthodox believers disapproved of nonconformist idealistic communities, such as the Montanists, who were seeking to preserve their identity against the Roman church or the eastern patriarchs. They were frequently accused of introducing dissolute sexual practices into their religious services. This became a familiar reproach in the history of religious strife. It was used against several sects during the Middle Ages and even by 'heathens' against the early Christians. And it is certainly true that there were fanatical religious movements on the borderlines of Christianity which did proclaim the sacramental character of physical love, continuing the orgiastic traditions of the fertility religions. Modern group sex has distant relations in the ritual sexual practices of certain underground sects, in the period of late antiquity as again in the Middle Ages between the twelfth and sixteenth centuries.

Youth movement characteristics can be seen during the twelfth and thirteenth centuries in three movements of significance to the development of the inner life of Europe: in the age of chivalry, with its poetry and its codes of behaviour; in a number of unorthodox Christian revival movements such as the Albigenses, and the early 'Brothers and Sisters of the Free Spirit'; and among the early Franciscans.

Young women formed the centre of the stylised courts of love in which the troubadours, the *trouvères,* the *Minnesänger* sang their praises as mistresses and heroines. But behind the court customs, the felicities (and infelicities) of chivalric love there was a hard core of reality. The landless younger sons of west European aristocrats were by

the nature of things rebels – first against their own
fathers, then against their spiritual fathers. Love
meant a rebellious, illicit relationship between a
young man and a young woman. Iseult got into bed
with young Tristan while her husband, King
Mark, was in church celebrating midnight mass.
This spirit of revolt, of rebellion against kings,
emperors and popes, against a monk-like asceticism,
echoes throughout the poetry of the age of chivalry,
from Provence to the Rhine.

Among the burned and drowned 'heretics', again
between Provence and the Rhine, there were, as
contemporary reports tell us, many very young
girls and boys. Laughing and singing, they marched
to their deaths with their spiritual brothers and
sisters. It was a spontaneous upsurge – observed
with amazement by their Church-supporting
enemies – of the joy, enthusiasm and contempt for
death that characterises youthful rebels and rebel
groups. In the early thirteenth century young
women and twelve-year-old girls fought beside their
husbands and brothers against the French crusaders'
army in Toulouse. Toulouse was for a long time the
bastion of the Albigenses, a religious revival movement outside the Christian Church. These young
militants fought with the same enthusiasm as young
girls in Budapest in 1956, and in Paris in 1968.

The early Franciscans possessed all the ardent
enthusiasm of a religious youth movement: a
refusal to compromise, and total rejection of the
existing pattern of power. All that is implied in the
order of poverty founded by St Francis of Assisi
and overthrown after a century of violent struggle.
'Left-wing' Franciscans extolled St Francis as the
Second Christ, the leader of a new era. These
Franciscans were burnt at the stake, or fled into
Africa and the wilds of Asia. The popes of the high
and late Middle Ages brought the Franciscan
youth movement to its knees. St Francis's own
order was racked for centuries by internal
squabbles.

Joan of Arc, the May Queen of France (whose
judges asked her whether she had danced with the

elves around the maypole on 1 May), drove the English from Orleans at the age of seventeen. Two years later, aged nineteen, she was burned as a witch. Joan was surrounded by young Franciscans. One of them, Brother Richard, named her the Holy Maid. The motto on her standard was Franciscan. Salvation, she proclaimed, would come from the people: the French king would be reborn as 'the son of France'. When her accusers, bribed by the English, slyly asked her, 'Does God hate the English?', she turned the question aside. She had already given her answer clearly enough in a missive addressed to the English king: 'In the name of God, our father in heaven, I have been sent to drive you bodily out of France.'

That is the language of the young generals of the French Revolution, and later of Napoleon. Modern European nationalism, promising salvation through the language and spirit of the people, owes not a little to the youthful enthusiasm of the great religious people's movements, such as the Hussites and the Lutherans.

The Reformation

At the age of fourteen Melanchthon left the university of Heidelberg in anger because he was not allowed, on account of his youth, to become a lecturer there. At the age of seventeen he was lecturing in Tübingen, and at twenty-one he was at Luther's side in Wittenberg. There the university had just been founded, and from central and eastern Europe it attracted first young professors and then students who combined to form a Lutheran movement. Its resemblance to a youth movement is unmistakable. Young curates, young nuns abandoned their spiritual fathers, married, became evangelical priests. A youthful ecstasy swept through the lands of the Holy Roman Empire, carrying the young people of Europe with it – in Poland, Bohemia (joining hands here with the earlier Hussites and with Waldenses elements), in the Austrian countries, Hungary, Croatia and the non-Islamic Balkans. Young Luther was the man who achieved most in his struggle with the 'brutal' super-father in Rome. A professor of philosophy at

The youthful Martin Luther achieves the great breakthrough against the 'old' world of Pope and Church. Woodcut by Lucas Cranach.

Wittenberg at the age of twenty-four, it was in the role of a rebellious professor of theology that ten years later he nailed his famous first demand for ecclesiastical reform to the church door. At the age of thirty-seven he published the three revolutionary works which questioned the validity of the existing Church structure down to its smallest detail: *On the Liberty of a Christian Man, On the Babylonian Captivity of the Church of God* and *An Address to the Nobility of the German Nation.* His left-wing supporters saw these also as an attack on the existing political establishment.

This youthful left-wing Lutheranism, which applied Luther's spiritually directed words literally to the prevailing political order, was defeated. It succumbed to the persecutions not only of Calvinists and Catholics, but of orthodox Lutherans as well. Thomas Müntzer, who began as Luther's disciple, later became his bitterest adversary, seeing him as a traitor both to God and to mankind. Müntzer, the preacher of Christian communism and leader of the peasants in the Peasants' War, was executed after defeat in battle in 1525 at the age of thirty-seven. Such is the fate of political religious rebels. Ernst Bloch and other convinced representatives of the New Left in our days see Müntzer as an early fighter for the world revolution that is to come – the revolution of mankind.

How radically the Lutheran 'cultural revolution' upset the order of things (much against the will of Melanchthon) can be seen in the complaints of Lutheran professors towards the end of the sixteenth century. Their students, they said, could no longer speak, write or think: they had become cultural barbarians. As a cure for this 'new barbarism' the Lutheran universities called in Spanish representatives of the new Jesuit school.

Ignatius de Loyola (born 1491) was no longer a young man when, after a period spent in the restrictive atmosphere of the college of Montaigu in Paris (which Erasmus remembered with repugnance and which helped to form Calcin), he founded the Society of Jesus in 1534. What he had begun in Montmartre with six friends comprised at the time of his death in 1556 one thousand members, a hundred and one houses and twelve provinces. In 1542 it penetrated into India, in 1549 into Japan and Brazil, in 1563 into China. With its six hundred colleges and academies it was the most powerful educational establishment in Europe throughout the seventeenth and eighteenth centuries. Its rapid rise can be explained only in the context of a political and religious youth movement: the angry young sons of the aristocracy, disgusted with the materialism, corruptness and decadence of their surroundings, abandoned their families and chose a new father – a spiritual father – for themselves. This was Ignatius de Loyola. And these young men, the padres of the Society of Jesus, in their turn, became the new spiritual fathers of ten generations of young sons – first from the aristocracy, later from the middle classes too.

Right-wing fathers of the Society of Jesus have had a hand in almost all the conservative and reactionary religious and political movements in Europe from the sixteenth to the twentieth centuries. Left-wing sons of Ignatius de Loyola have sought out their opponents, discussed their differences with Lutherans, Calvinists and other 'heretics', founded in Paraguay the first prototype of a Utopian Christian state and sought a symbiosis with the cultures of India and China.

Active participants in the world youth movement in our own time include in Germany Lutheran student priests; in the United States young Protestant and Catholic theologians and priests (among them some Jesuits), demonstrating for civil

rights and against the war in Vietnam; in Spain, young curates protesting and campaigning against the Franco regime; in Latin America, bishops, priests and members of religious orders defying dictatorships in Argentina, Brazil and other states. This widely differentiated political and religious youth movement within the church could never have come into being were it not for those earlier Christian youth movements. Crushed, repressed, dissolved, absorbed they may have been, but they

A battle scene from the war of the Hussites, 1420–1431.

left behind them traces of which we, in the final third of the twentieth century, are reminded throughout the world.

Thomas Chatterton, 'the marvellous boy who perished in his pride', committed suicide at the age of seventeen.

Youth and the great revolution

In July 1770 the poet Thomas Chatterton wrote to his sister: 'I must be among the great. State matters suit me better than commercial'. Shortly afterwards, in a fit of despair, he committed suicide – at the age of seventeen. Convinced that the young poet, the young visionary, had a political mission, he symbolised the loneliness of youth in a state of deep spiritual unrest. Chatterton was the first of many young poets, painters and artists who were to commit suicide in the nineteenth and twentieth centuries. In him can be seen all the anger, grief, rebellion that found expression through the poets of the following generation – Byron, Shelley, Keats, Blake. They recognised themselves in Chatterton, as later generations in England and America between the years 1965 and 1970 were to recognise themselves in Shelley, Byron and Blake.

In 1774 Goethe published *The Sorrows of Young Werther*. In Germany, France, Poland, Hungary and Italy young people hailed the book as a revolutionary proclamation against all the conventions of a fossilised society, dominated by aristocrats who refused the young sons of the lower orders social equality and the chance to improve their position. The old Roman quarrel between plebeians and patricians arose again in a new form.

For the people of its own generation *Werther* was not merely a sentimental masterpiece that precipitated a wave of suicides among young people. The young Napoleon carried it in his knapsack when he went to Egypt. Students in Russia, Poland and Hungary saw it as a call to action against foreign dominators and their aristocratic and ecclesiastical supporters inside the state. It was a call to the individual, to the free God-communing heart, *within* the context of a general rising.

In the period around 1770 a broad front of young

Title page of the *Songs of Innocence* by William Blake.

people stood ranged in Germany against the three hundred German princes; against the priests in their empty churches; and against the obsolete universities and schools with their pernicious restrictions of thought and feeling. The Holy Roman Empire was wasting away in a vast number of little states whose tyrannical overlords, half a century after the death of the Sun King, still aped his artificial heaven of Versailles in their vulgar and libidinous festivities. The true revolution began with a rebellion of the heart, a new sensibility of thought and feeling, and it was with unions, with brotherhoods, that these sensitive young people

The young Goethe;
a contemporary
engraving.

sought to combat the decadence of their fathers. The first fraternity of rebellious young poets, *der Hain* (the Grove), was founded in 1772 at Göttingen, a university town strongly influenced by the English school of Enlightenment. Rousseau's *Du Contrat social* of 1762 acted like a fanfare on these restless young Germans. 'Man was born free, but everywhere he lies in chains. . .'. As their leader they invoked Prometheus, who stole fire from the gods. Maximilian Klinger, whose play *Sturm und Drang* (Storm and Stress) gave its name to the first real German youth movement, spoke of Prometheus as the 'unrecognised son of God', and Herder, the

Edict of the Elector of Saxony's Commissioner of Books forbidding the distribution of Goethe's book *Werther*; issued in 1775.

young Goethe, the young Schiller, Beethoven and Schubert celebrated him in word and song. In 1965 Prometheus was invoked again – in Berkeley, California.

In 1777 Duke Karl Eugen of Württemberg had the highly talented poet, composer and journalist Schubart seized and thrown into prison for 'blasphemous libel against almost all the crowned heads in the world'. For ten years Schubart lay

Left Jean-Jacques Rousseau (1712–78) after a portrait by Latour. 'Man is born free, but everywhere he lies in fetters', wrote the French philosopher in his *Contrat Social*. Restless German intellectuals reacted to this sentence as to a trumpet call and in 1781 the young German poet Friedrich von Schiller prefaced his drama *The Robbers* with *In Tyrannos*. **Right** As a military cadet at Bosperwald near Stuttgard he reads his play secretly to his friends: a sketch by his fellow-cadet Heidehoff.

confined in the dungeons of Hohenasperg, without either trial or sentence. One of Karl Eugen's 'subjects', the twenty-one-year-old Schiller, had Schubart's fate in mind when, in 1781, he wrote his play *Die Räuber* (The Robbers) and printed on the title-page the motto *In tyrannos* (Against Tyrants). Schiller could look back on a harsh and frustrated childhood. Brought up in a bigoted, lower middle-class home, he had been sent at the age of fourteen, at the duke's command, to a military school where he was to be trained as an army doctor. It was a hard school, and to the young boy it was hell. Here he began to write – as an escape to freedom.

A German prince later told Goethe that, had he been God and had he known that the creation of the world would also have implied the creation of Schiller's *Die Räuber*, he would have left the world unmade. This German prince was certainly right in

perceiving that Schiller's youthful work (and Goethe's too) sought to demolish the whole existing structure of power in Europe, whether political, social or religious.

Die Räuber, first produced on 13 January 1782, made Schiller the acknowledged spokesman of the younger generation in Germany. For attending a performance of *Die Räuber* in Mannheim without permission he was sentenced by the duke to fourteen days' imprisonment and forbidden to have any communication with the world abroad ('abroad' beginning only a few miles away from Stuttgart). Forbidden, under threat of dismissal, from writing any further plays, Schiller fled from Württemberg. While 'abroad' (in Thuringia), he wrote a further play *Kabale und Liebe* (Intrigue and Love, but also known in English as *Luise Miller*), which is a tragedy about a love destroyed by corrupt princes and their henchmen. In the course of this play the prince's mistress, Lady Milford, is told by a servant

English engraving, entitled: 'An enslaved French Republican'.

Above: Camille Desmoulins, aged 29, makes his famous speech before the Palais-Royal, Paris, on 12 July 1789. Contemporary engraving by Duplessis-Bertaux. **Left:** F.M. Arouet, known as Voltaire, chooses his new name in order to dissociate himself from his hated father. **Overleaf:** a revolutionary tribunal in session during the 'reign of terror' 1793–4.

about the sale of mercenaries. At that time German princes had sold thousands of their 'subjects' to the British, to be used as soldiers against the colonists in America. In 1781 one of these human sacrifices had been the seventeen-year-old student of theology, J. G. Seume. In his autobiography Seume describes his deportation to America to serve as an English soldier in the War of Independence against the Americans. Seume returned from America a convinced democrat and later had a significant influence on Nietzsche.

The French Revolution

The year 1789 saw the beginning of the French Revolution. On 3 August in that year Jean Paul proclaimed: 'God is dead.' This was to haunt young poets and thinkers in France, Germany, Spain, Poland and Russia throughout the nineteenth century. The poet Friedrich Richter, who took the name Jean Paul in honour of Rousseau, announced his vision at first only obliquely under the title 'Dead Shakespeare's lament to a dead congregation in church that there is no God'. But the later version is entitled 'The dead Christ reveals to the world that there is no God'.

Youth movements, above all in Europe, have always been closely connected with the problem of religious faith (which goes beyond the crisis of religion, of the church, of a ruling order based on an alliance of church and state). Young people find it impossible to believe in the old idea of God. Where is he? Does he ally himself with old men to slaughter his sons on the battlefields of reactionary wars?

In 1789 Jean Paul was twenty-five years old. In 1784, five years before the start of the French Revolution, Schiller had launched his periodical *Rheinische Thalia* with a revolutionary manifesto. He was, he said, no longer prepared to appeal to any throne 'other than that of the human soul'. He saw himself as 'a citizen of the universe, who will take any member of the human race into his family and guard the interests of all with brotherly love'. This was Schiller's German version of the motto *Liberté, Egalité, Fraternité*.

The French National Assembly made the young

Terror accompanies the revolution; **Left:** an eleven-year-old 'patriot' from Marseilles. **Below:** Robespiere addressing a gathering of Jacobins on 26 July 1794.

Schiller an honorary citizen of their new society guaranteeing the rights of men. For all the differences of their outcome, the youth movements of France and Germany were parallel in kind. The revolution of German youth may have been only within the heart and mind, but – through Hegel – it struck sparks in the nineteenth and twentieth centuries. The young Karl Marx was, above all, a product of left-wing romanticism, the German youth movement that led up to the revolution of 1848. The French youth movement led straight into revolution.

In 1789 Bonaparte, Madame de Staël and Chateaubriand were all twenty years old. Hölderlin, Hegel, Schelling and Schlegel were their exact contemporaries. Schiller, Robespierre and Danton were all in their thirtieth year, while Antoine de Saint-Just was twenty-two. All these deeply disturbed young people shared the same spiritual fathers: Rousseau and Voltaire.

It is a characteristic of discontented youth to seek new fathers: spiritual, political, religious, artistic fathers, or gurus. (It happened in Germany in 1922, when young fatherless students, returning from the Great War, went to the universities to seek not professors, but spiritual and political fathers. It happened in the United States in 1965 and in 1970.) The spiritual fathers chosen in the years 1770–90 by young Frenchmen and young Germans (and in the nineteenth century by young Russians, Poles, Italians) were the first to play the role assumed in our days by such figures as Hegel, Marx, Herbert Marcuse and Reich.

François-Marie Arouet (1694–1778) changed his name to Voltaire out of hatred for his father. Voltaire's fight was directed, above all, against the old gods, kings and priests of old Europe. He wanted a *roi plus doux*, a gentler god-king than the brutal judges and generals of the existing order. 'Why do we all persecute one another?' he asked in *La Loi Naturelle* (1752). 'Are we not brothers, the children of a single God? Bowed down as we are beneath the load of our sins, let us help one another to carry the burden.' In Voltaire's appeal to reason can be seen all the motives that were later, in the works of Camus and Sartre, to capture the imagination of French youth in the period 1944–55.

Jean-Jacques˙ Rousseau (1712–78) told young people that the new world of the future could be built only by simple and truthful human beings without party bias, putting trust in the sincerity of their own individual hearts. Rousseau later became the spiritual father of a 'people's democracy'. 'Whoever seeks to refashion a people must know himself capable of changing human nature, re-shaping every individual.' He was to be one of the fathers of a rational political democracy and of that mystic form of nationalism to which so many young Europeans fell victim in the nineteenth century and the beginning of the twentieth.

A spirit of enthusiasm filled the hearts of young aristocrats, bourgeois sons, writers, artists, budding priests on the eve of the French Revolution. Even village priests were reported to have been seen standing with bowed heads in the street as Voltaire's coffin was borne past on the way to Paris. There was a feeling of renewal: the world was to be rejuvenated, cleansed in an action that would wash away all the evil, the spiritual and political sores, the dirt, the ugliness and the brutality of the 'old world'. French youth, in alliance with the young people of the earth, would usher in the new era, helped by men and women of an older generation who had remained young in spirit. Something of the enthusiasm which filled the proclamations, pamphlets and speeches of that time was to startle the citizens of Paris once again – in May 1968.

The French Revolution

Perhaps the most dramatic embodiment of the spirit of these young revoutionaries was Saint-Just, who went to his death at the age of twenty-six in 1794, along with Robespierre. Saint-Just was reported by contemporaries to have held his own head proudly high as he demanded the execution of the King in November 1792, of the Girondins in July 1793, the Hébertists in March 1794 and finally Danton in the same month. The enemy must be destroyed before the social order could be reborn. Saint-Just's belief in this tragic necessity recurred again among youthful radicals in Russia in the period 1860–90, and in both America and Europe in the years 1960–70.

Saint-Just was the first genius of political romanticism. He combined the ideas of both Pascal and Nietzsche in his longing for a heroic, dangerous life 'between deadly dangers and immortality'. Great men did not die in their beds. 'It is only for people who are frightened of death that things are difficult', he said. 'For people who wish to rebel and to do what is right there is no time for sleep, except in the grave.' It is the longing for death combined with a belief in the future – a combination to be met again in Czechoslovakia and France, in the years 1968–70, when schoolchildren and students set fire to themselves. 'The individual being, faced with the necessity of parting both from the world and from himself, casts his anchor into the future and embraces the generations to come, who are innocent of the sins of the present.' 'I despise the dust of which I am composed, and which speaks to you (through me). This dust can be persecuted and put to death. But I defy you to snatch away this independent life I have given myself in the heavens and the coming centuries.' In an early poem Saint-Just wrote: 'I shall go my way without weapons, without defence, followed by hearts and not by hangmen.' Later, Algerian, Tunisian, Arab and Vietnamese students (among them the young Ho Chi Minh) took their lead, together with young writers, sociologists and students in France and in South America, from Saint-Just.

The words of Camille Desmoulins (1760–94), who delivered in front of the Palais Royal the speech that unleashed the French Revolution, are full of revolutionary fire. 'What distinguishes the Republic from the monarchy? One thing only: the freedom to write and speak.' 'What is the best weapon the free peoples have to protect themselves from despotism? The freedom of the press. What is the second best? The freedom of the press. And the third? The freedom of the press.' 'The freedom that comes from heaven is no operatic illusion. It is also not a red cap, a filthy shirt or a tattered robe. Freedom is happiness, reason, equality, justice, the declaration of human rights, your admirable constitution!'

Compare the language of Saint-Just and Desmoulins with that of Daniel Cohn-Bendit in 1968. Though deliberately damped down, Cohn-Bendit's

Napoleon, in Schönbrunn, interrogates Stabs, a German student who tried to assassinate him.

nevertheless breathes the same spirit of enthusiasm.

On 1 April 1794, four days before his execution, Desmoulins wrote to his adored wife: 'You see in me an example of man's barbarism and ingratitude. . . . I dreamed of a republic that would appeal to *all* men. I could never have believed that human beings could be so brutal and unjust.'

It would be absurd to consider the French Revolution to have been nothing more than a youth movement. But it contained in its complexities many elements of a youth movement. And it is the fate of revolutionary youth movements to flare up suddenly, in bright, upright flames, which are then stamped out, or die down of their own accord – sometimes both together. There is something of the carnival spirit in them. The Carnival King – normally a slave – reigns for a day or a week. All the usual patterns of authority are reversed in games, dances, orgies. Passions and instincts are given free rein. Like characters on a stage, the victims are tried and marched to the guillotine between cheering crowds.

But somewhere in the crowd, or in the wings, the 'new man' is waiting. One day he will discipline these young people and turn them to his own use. Napoleon. Or another liberator – a *Duce*, a *Führer*. That too is part of the historic fate of all youth movements which have no clearly defined limits or objectives.

The Romantic reaction

Great Britain was the birthplace of European romanticism. And romanticism was the first youth movement to sweep through Europe in successive waves up to 1848 and beyond. Great Britain was also the birthplace of the industrial revolution. Here the 'two nations', of which Friedrich Engels and Disraeli were later to speak, clashed together with a harshness and brutality which encouraged thinking young people to believe that the world revolution would begin in Britain.

But in Great Britain the preservative instinct is also strong. Nowhere else in Europe do medieval traditions of justice, politics and social order linger on so persistently.

King George III, wasting away in illness, insanity and blindness, once asked an Eton schoolboy on one of his clearer days whether he had not recently staged a rebellion. Risings and disturbances in English schools were not uncommon in the first years of the French Revolution. In 1793 Winchester College was held in occupation by its pupils for two days. The Red Flag was flown on the Middle Gate. In 1818 troops had to be called in to deal with recalcitrant pupils.

In August 1819 a meeting of some sixty thousand people in St Peter's Field, Manchester, was broken up by force, leaving many dead and injured. It was a triumph for political reaction under the leadership of the Duke of Wellington, the strong man behind the Tories until his death in 1852. Shelley, a refugee from England, wrote his poem *The Mask of Anarchy* in Italy:

> I met Murder in the way –
> He had a mask like Castlereagh.
> Very smooth he looked, yet grim;
> Seven blood-hounds followed him:
> All were fat: and well they might

England was the motherland of European Romanticism. **Right** Lord Byron, who had fled to exile in Italy. **Below**: John Keats (study by B. R. Haydan) and **Opposite**: Percy B. Shelley, who drowned in 1822, gave aim and direction to rebellious youth.

Be in admirable plight,
For one by one, and two by two,
He tossed them human hearts to chew
Which from his wider cloak he drew.

(As British Foreign Secretary Castlereagh, from 1814 until his suicide in 1822, attempted to form a conservative bloc on the Continent, with the object of keeping a check, as occasion arose, on both France and Russia.)

Commenting in 1969 on Shelley, Keats and Byron in their fight against the established order, Stephen Spender wrote of the lines quoted above: 'Any young American poet, reflecting on the bombing of North Vietnam, might write in similar vein of any American presidential candidate of the 1968 November election.'

'England! awake! awake! awake!' It is a recurring theme in Blake's work. Unlike the call *Deutschland, erwache!* (Germany, awake), which – though perverted in 1933 – had its roots in German left-wing pietism, Blake's 'England, awake!' had its origin in a sermon of John Wesley, a great influence in his life. Blake, who in the years 1955–70 was to be adopted by young Englishmen and Americans as

the prophet of their vision of a better future, saw
both heaven and hell in England. He looked with
horror on human misery in London, saw men
abused by court, church, state and university. The
divine gift of imagination was stifled by the universities, as England was stifled by the factories, the
'dark Satanic mills'.

> O Earth, O Earth, return!
> Arise from out the dewy grass;
> Night is worn,
> And the morn
> Rises from the slumberous mass.

Blake, in the midst of his English Jacobin friends,
saw world revolution as a total experience. It was
something that would transform all national, social
and religious institutions and liberate both sexes to
new sensual experience. It was Blake who urged

Thomas Paine to escape to France in 1792 in order to avoid arrest. Blake's poem *The French Revolution*, set up in type in 1791, was never published.

In the years between Blake's *Songs of Innocence* (1789) and the death of Shelley in 1822 English romanticism was at its height. It flowered with Wordsworth, Coleridge and Keats – and above all Byron, in whom the ideals of the French Revolution remained alive even in the years of despair, vexation and boredom.

Shelley was twenty-seven when he completed his *Prometheus Unbound* in the late summer of 1819. For Shelley, as for Goethe and Beethoven, Prometheus was the symbol of man's creative power. Prometheus fought against evil, hunger, sickness, need in the reign of Jupiter and his old kings and priests. In his poems Shelley proclaimed his vision of the future, where earth would no longer be a hell. Love and freedom, health and happiness would prevail, and women would stand at the side of men, 'changed to all which once they dared not be, Yet being now, made earth like heaven. . . .'.

Poets, as Shelley proclaimed in his *Defence of Poetry*, are the unacknowledged legislators of the world. The great poets of humanity, Moses, David, Solomon, Isaiah, Christ and the apostles, summon the divine fire, cherish it and destroy evil, sin and death in its flames. It is this belief in creative fantasy that binds the young men of the first cultural revolution, the great period of European romanticism, with the young people of 1960–70.

Byron (1788–1824) was hailed by Goethe, Mazzini, by Germans, Poles, Russians, Frenchmen, Italians, Spaniards as a leader of young Europe. Pushkin conceived his *Eugène Onegin* as a reply to Byron's *Don Juan*.

> For I will teach, if possible, the stones
> To rise against earth's tyrants. Never let it
> Be said that we still truckle unto thrones;
> But ye – our children's children! think how we
> Show'd *what things were* before the world was free!
>   (*Don Juan*, Canto VIII, CXXXV)

This – to apply the language of our own time – is

a protest song. Byron openly attacked the regime of George IV and the Duke of Wellington. He urged the people to send 'the bald-coot bully', Tsar Alexander, and all the kings and emperors of the Holy Alliance to Senegal to be sold as slaves:

Teach them that 'sauce for goose is sauce for gander', and ask them how *they* like to be in thrall.

Byron believed that men would rise from their chains, whether imposed or self-imposed. On 19 April 1824, Easter Monday, he died in Missolonghi, having sacrificed both his money and his health in the Greek struggle for independence. He knew that the awakening people of Greece (forerunners of others in our own day) were in danger of tearing themselves to pieces in a bloody civil war, yet he did not draw back. For all its miseries, he saw the Greek struggle as a necessary step along man's path

All over Europe patriots were being persecuted by reactionary forces. A.Gisbert's painting shows the execution of the Spanish rebel Don José Maria Torrijos and his companions in 1831.

European Romanticism

to a hopeful future and a better way of life.

The period of European romanticism, 1800–48, was the period of youth in revolt. The French Revolution had aroused very great hopes: the period of Napoleon and the great reaction that set in after 1815 plunged these young people into a mood of deep despair.

On New Year's Eve the poet Friedrich Hölderlin wrote to his brother Karl: 'The clock is just striking

midnight, and the year 1799 begins. I wish a happy year to you and all our people. And then a happy, great new century for Germany and the world.' In 1793 Hölderlin had written, 'My love is the whole human race. Not indeed the slavish, dull, spoiled part of it that we only too often meet, even in our limited experience. But even in them I love the potential of greatness and beauty. *I love the human race of the coming centuries.*' And in 1797,

'My consolation is that fermentation and disintegration in any form must necessarily lead either to destruction or to reorganisation. *But since there is no such thing as destruction, the youth of the world must rise up again from our putrefaction. I believe in a future revolution of feelings and conceptions that will make everything that has gone before blush with shame.* And Germany can perhaps provide a lot towards it.'

Friedrich Hegel (**opposite**) surrounded by his pupils. Schelling and Hölderlin were the accepted teachers of German students during the epoch of Romanticism, and their leaders in the battle against politically repressive forces. **Right**: Students leaving Göttingen in protest in 1831.

The first Young Germany, around the year 1800, was based on the idea of fraternity. Its leading lights were Hölderlin, Hegel, Schelling, Novalis and the brothers Schlegel, who ran the periodical *Athenäum*, influential organ of the Romantic Movement. In the eighteen-forties there was to be another *Athenäum*, and on its threshold a young left-wing Hegelian, the young Karl Marx. . . .

In the south-west corner of Germany in particular the French Revolution inspired the rise of secret societies, composed of German Jacobins. In the fight against the French Revolution and Napoleon, students allied with freedom fighters to wage the 'wars of liberation' that took place between 1809 and 1813. A meeting on the Wartburg in 1817 – the first mass-gathering of a European (in this case a specifically German) youth movement – brought together radical young Germans, idealistic nationalists hoping for salvation through the collective German soul, and various other liberal, conservative and nationalistic elements.

At this meeting students burned books. In 1933 there were to be other outbreaks of book-burning by students in German university towns.

The first political murder in Germany to occur within the framework of a youth movement perverted to fanaticism was the assassination of the playwright Kotzebue in 1819. Kotzebue was suspected of being a Russian spy, but in fact he had been doing no more than many other politicians, princes and writers in German lands, who for several centuries had been earning pensions for themselves in the service of various foreign rulers.

Behind the murder, which was committed by a student named Sand, stood the cold and calculating figure of Karl Follen, a teacher, and the leader of a group called the *Giessener Schwarzen* (the Black Sect of Giessen). Follen's role was comparable in many respects with that of some university lecturers in France and the United States in our own recent times. The *Giessener Schwarzen* constituted one of the most radical groups within the German students association. Humanism and tolerance in the spirit of Goethe were anathema to it.

Heinrich Heine saw in the book-burnings of 1817 an augury of things to come. 'People who burn books,' he said, 'will also turn to burning people.' A hundred years later his prophecy came true. Heine also had something to say about the *Giessener Schwarzen*: 'At the very time when nearly all nationalities were vanishing, there arose a black sect which indulged in the most foolish dreams of nationhood, and even more foolish plans for realising them. . . . They were able to determine the precise genealogical grade at which a person became eligible, under the new order, for removal from this world. But they could not agree on the method of execution. Some considered the sword would be the most truly German way, while others thought the guillotine would do, since it was, after all, a German invention.' 'Where does Germanic man begin? And where does he leave off? In a beer cellar in Göttingen I once (1820) found myself observing with admiration the thoroughness with which my Germanic friends set about preparing their proscription lists in anticipation of the day when they would assume power. All people with a scrap of French, Jewish or Slav blood in them, back to the

A wide spectrum of the German Romantic youth-movement joined forces in German student organizations: a contemporary English caricature of student life in Germany.

The brain behind the assassin Sand, **right** was the coldly intellectual private lecturer Follen of Giessen, **far right**.

seventh generation, were condemned to exile.'

German youth movements of the radical right wing were to think that way again in 1920 and 1933. And we encounter a similar fanaticism after 1945, above all in coloured youth movements in Africa and North America and among Mao's 'Young Guards', who reject all connections with white people as obscene.

The Wartburg meeting in 1817 was held under the patronage of Goethe's friend, Grand Duke Karl August. It laid the foundations for the *Allgemeine Deutsche Burschenschaft*, a students' organisation covering the whole of Germany, which came into existence in Jena in October of the following year. The *Deutsche Burschenschaft*, which provided the model for German youth movements of all political and non-political persuasions in the years 1900–33, brought a number of very varied elements together, grouped around a radical right wing, a radical left wing and a broad, relatively non-political centre. *Burschenschaft* members like Arnold Ruge (Marx's youthful friend who became an enemy in later years) developed into staunch democrats, radicals and republicans. They sowed the seeds from which the 1848 revolution grew, and their spirit lingered on to give life to the national liberal movement of the German middle classes in the late nineteenth century.

A radical right-wing group grew up in Jena around the university lecturer Jakob Friedrich

Fries, who gained a hypnotic influence over a generation of young Germans in which fanaticism was ever on the increase.

The resistance of the German princes and their governments to the Young Germany movement succeeded in the years after 1835 in splitting up the German youth movements. On 10 December 1835 the German Bundestag passed a resolution calling on the governments of all its member states to take immediate steps against writers and publishers of literature bearing the Young Germany stamp, in particular Heinrich Heine, Karl Gutzkow, Heinrich

German students burn the works of 'reactionaries' at the Wartburg festival of 1817.

Laube, Ludolf Wienbarg and Theodor Mundt. The reason given was that these Young Germany writers were 'using a humorous and easily readable literary form to attack the Christian religion in a most insolent manner, to denigrate the existing social order and to destroy discipline and morality.' These efforts to undermine the 'foundations of law and order' must immediately be brought to a halt by the combined efforts of all member governments.

D

This Bundestag resolution of 1835 can still be regarded as an excellent model for repressive measures available to governments of both right and left, who aim to protect the state from 'youthful excesses' and 'rebellions' and to suppress all intellectual, literary and political opposition. In the German states it succeeded, up to 1848 and beyond, in creating – through arrests, denunciations, trials, prison sentences, banishings and intimidations – a high degree of bitterness and despair; and thus forced a resigned generation of young people to conform to the 'law and order' of the existing regime.

The word 'romantic' does more to obscure than to throw light on the great youth movement that swept like wildfire through Europe between the years 1789 and 1848. This, the first cultural revolution in Europe, seized hold of young French minds in the years 1810–20, took root in Italy and Spain in the next ten years, then, moving into Hungary, Poland and Russia, spread out into Holland, Sweden and Portugal.

The purpose of the movement was defined by the Spaniard José Larra (who, like so many of these young revolutionaries, ended by taking his own life): 'Freedom of literature, as of the arts, as of industry, as of trade, as of conscience – that is the slogan of our epoch, that is *our* slogan!' Freedom means the liberation of the imagination, of feeling, of the emotional impulses stifled in school and university. It means release of the sexual urge, liberation from the straitjacket of classical forms and academic dictatorship. (In the Paris rising of May 1968 art students were in the front line.) Freedom means liberation of the religious spirit from the domination of the church; of the critical spirit from the domination of professors; liberation of women. Freedom means, in fact, liberation from all inner and outward dictatorships.

Repressions designed to deprive people of the chance to live these freedoms, led to pessimism and melancholy and a refuge in drug-taking. Release, the extension of consciousness, was sought in artificial paradises, in dreams and intoxicated visions which the outer world could not provide. This 'flight into night' was much more – in 1830, in 1840 and again 120 years later – than merely a literary fashion. Several of the most gifted, most sensitive young people paid for it with their lives.

Diaries and poems written by young people throughout Europe bore witness to suffering, indignation and a sense of hopelessness. Mameli and La Vista died at the age of twenty-two, Turrisi-Colonna, Manuel de Cabanyes and Juan Francisco Carbo aged twenty-five. Petöfi, the Hungarian poet of freedom whom Hungarian students invoked in 1956, was killed in battle at the age of twenty-six. Lermontov lost his life in a duel at the age of twenty-seven. Radičević was twenty-nine when he died; Tristan Corbière and Pablo Piferrer thirty; José Semis, Wesiliwski, Nievo, Shelley, Larra, Emindescu, Chopin, Stagnelius were in their thirty-second year. Throughout Europe, from Paris to St Petersburg, a long succession of young poets, writers and artists ended their lives in madness and suicide.

Between 1819 and 1823 Francisco Goya painted his huge and terrible *Saturn Consuming his Sons* – a portrayal of the forces of reaction, above all in Europe. Poets and artists in Russia, Poland, Hungary, France and Spain expressed in the years 1830–70 the terrible suspicion that their fathers – in the shape of tsars, emperors, kings, priests and statesmen – were intent on slaughtering their rebellious sons: preferably by sending them to war, but, failing that, in internal battles.

Periods of hope and hopelessness followed one another like waves in the years 1830–48, the era of Young Europe. Mazzini formulated the programme of his Young Italy in 1831. In the same year Towianski left Poland for Paris. In the years up to 1918 Paris became a place of refuge for exiles from Poland, Hungary, Germany and the southern Slav countries (also from 1900 for restless Americans). Revolutionary hope combined with a spirit of messianic nationalism. Among the awakening peoples (at that time the Balkans played the role that in our time is assumed by China and Cuba) 'brothers' rose up against their 'fathers'. From 1830 onwards there was a widespread feeling that the old regime – the tsar in Russia, the sultan in the Balkans, the emperor in Vienna, the pope in Rome – was on the point of collapse. In political songs the revolutionary poets of Russia, Poland, Hungary, Serbia, Greece and Italy proclaimed their great hope that the liberation of their country would point the way to the liberation of all mankind. The best of these poets, like Petöfi, put the accent on a combination of inner and outer freedom. The Hungarian people must first get rid of its feudal overlords: otherwise liberation from Vienna, from the soldiers of the emperor and the tsar, would lose all its meaning.

In June 1848 a mass meeting of students in Eisenach set about the task of reorganising the universities. 'Fellow students, the revolutions of this year have shaken the foundations of all institutions, including our own. Revolution is the birthplace of our new university system!' As Gerhard Linne has pointed out, many of the proposals discussed in Eisenach look today, in our own days of university reform, like a bold sally into the future.

The German rising of 1848 was crushed. By 1854 more than three hundred thousand Germans, among them a select group of young revolutionaries, had emigrated, most of them to America.

The rising power of the United States in the nineteenth century was profoundly affected by this leavening of German youth. America was the country that profited most from the collapse of this democratic movement in the centre of Europe, in which a restive young generation had played a leading role.

Karl Follen, the university lecturer who had been behind the political assassination of Kotzebue, became a professor at Harvard.

Boy Scouts and Christian Youth Associations

Most of the youth movements dealt with so far have been movements of more-or-less spontaneous young rebellion against established values. But the early twentieth century saw the growth on an unprecedented scale of another phenomenon: youth movements set up by representatives of the existing order to harness the idealism of the young for the purification and *preservation* of existing values. The most important were the boy scout movement and the Christian youth associations.

The Boy Scouts

In the years of ominous calm between the Boer War and the First World War Major-General Robert Baden-Powell, hero of Mafeking and inspector-general of the cavalry, created the scout movement. His own schoolboy experiences at Charterhouse, holiday camps with his brothers and a soldier's life in India and South Africa provided the pattern for his first experimental camp, which was set up on Brownsea Island in Poole Harbour in 1907. Here Baden-Powell put into effect the ideas which he defined in his book *Scouting for Boys* in the following year. Boys were encouraged to organise themselves in natural groups of six or seven under a patrol leader of their own age. They were trained in certain simple techniques, such as map-reading, signalling, knot-tying and first aid. They pledged themselves to do their duty towards God and their sovereign, and to help other people at all times – in other words, to introduce a note of chivalry into a brutal world that was fast forgetting the meaning of neighbourly love.

Baden-Powell's initial intention was simply to inject his principles into the youth movements already in existence, but with extraordinary rapidity the scouts blossomed into a separate movement of their own. The movement spread first to Chile, Canada, Australia, New Zealand and South Africa, and by 1910 it was also established in Sweden, France, Norway, Mexico, Argentina and the United States of America.

The scout movement was designed originally for boys between the ages of eleven and fourteen, but Baden-Powell soon saw the necessity for widening the age range. For younger boys he created the wolf cubs (called 'cub scouts' in the USA), who had their own uniform and training as well as a separate motto: 'Do your best'. Rudyard Kipling's *Jungle Books* provided the inspiration for this movement, both in Britain and abroad. Older boys became senior scouts and rover scouts (in France 'raiders' and in the United States 'explorers').

Understandably, the boy scout movement suffered a setback during the First World War, but from 1920 onwards it made great strides throughout the world. Sir Robert (later Lord) Baden-Powell was acknowledged everywhere as Chief Scout and enthusiastically cheered and feted at all world scout jamborees. The various national organisations were autonomous, but they all recognised an international headquarters, situated originally in London and since 1958 in Ottawa. In the Sixties there were more than eight and a half million active scouts throughout the world. The ideals of the world scout movement are based on a spirit of self-reliance and responsibility among young people (mainly boys: the girl guide movement, a later development, played a subsidiary role). Its principles are selflessness and helpfulness, good-fellowship both at home and abroad.

If there is any hint of tragedy to be found in the scout movement, it must be sought less in the fact that fascistic, communistic and other totalitarian regimes at various times placed a ban on it, than in the fact that other regimes have tended to exploit it for national purposes – particularly in times of war. Like the Red Cross (the true story of whose activities during the Second World War, including those curious visits to German concentration camps, has yet to be told), the scout movement is the victim of its own political abstinence – that anaemic refusal

to take an active part in a dynamic peace movement. What could eight and a half million impassioned young scouts not achieve, if they were to apply their lively humanitarian principles actively to the political (but not party political) scene in the interests of the family of man?

Like all other youth movements which were set up, led and are still being led from above, the scouts have shared the frustrating fate of being pressed into service by larger organisations, both political and religious – in other words, of being used as human material.

The Christian youth associations reached the height of their activity, particularly in Germany,

An open-air devotional service of the Christliche Pfad-finderschaft (Christian Scouts).

58

In many countries religious youth movements and scout movements became closely linked; a bible-reading at a scouts' camp.

The Christian youth associations

during the first thirty years of the twentieth century.

From the very beginning German youth movements tended to display vague feelings of religious inspiration, which found expression in various ways: in a worship of Nature, in Germanic evocations and romantic longings. Young people sought God in Nature or in Eros, and temporarily believed themselves to have found him there. The original *Wandervogel* movement was imbued with a spirit of Protestantism that saw Luther as Germany's 'free man' and had nothing but contempt for church bureaucracy. Now and again, from about 1920 onwards, these young enthusiasts took possession of the cathedral in Erfurt for a day. Werner Helwig, one of the founding fathers of the German youth movement, recalls in his book *Die Blaue Blume des Wandervogels* (1960) a 'crusade of joyfulness' initiated by Muck Lamberty and his troop from Thuringia during the Twenties. A lay sermon was preached in Erfurt Cathedral on the theme, 'We believe in youth, the bearer of God's own gift of creation'. Young Protestants sang their own hymns – but Roman Catholic songs as well.

It was a manifestation of undirected religious fervour which the elders of the established churches could neither appreciate nor comprehend. But over the young men of the church, theologians longing for means to prove the living relevance of their chosen faith, it exercised a powerful fascination.

For German Catholicism it represented a moment of destiny, and for Romano Guardini, a Roman Catholic priest, philosopher and youth leader, a starting point from which he gained, in the years from 1924 onwards, a unique position of influence over the Catholic youth movement in Germany and the new intellectual movement that stemmed from it. Right up to his death in 1969 Guardini retained his hold, however indirect and personally unobtrusive, over a select group of Catholics in Federal Germany whose critical outlook owed much to memories of their stirring youthful past.

Beside his activities as co-publisher of the periodical *Schildgenossen* from 1924 to 1941 and leader of the youth centre Rothenfels from 1926 to 1939, Guardini spent nine years, from 1924 to 1933, as leader of the Catholic youth movement known as Quickborn. Described as a movement based on principles of abstinence, Quickborn had been founded in 1909 at the same time as the boy scout movement in Britain. Its ideals were set out by Guardini in a declaration published in 1921. 'Rambling is a form of life. Each is dependent on himself and his companions. All decisions must be made on the spot. Rambling is a quest for the people and for a life within the people.' The Quick-born movement regarded itself as part of a great community of peoples and the best possible counter-attack against a socialism 'based solely on the rootless masses in the cities'.

Undoubtedly successful as Quickborn and other Catholic youth movements in Germany were in breeding a generation of sensitive and spiritually-minded personalities who were to play an important part in the early formative years of the Federal Republic, all of them suffered from one fatal weakness. Their members – apart from a few exceptions – failed to develop a positive individual attitude towards the realities of a pluralistic society, towards democracy and urban civilisation in an industrial age. Though individual groups sought by inner resistance to hold back the swift advance of National Socialism, these young Catholics were as powerless as their Protestant brothers to control it. The fatal similarity of their declared aims and beliefs – the crusading spirit of nationalism, the longing for identification with a mystical 'German people', the distrust of the 'wicked West', the profoundly irrational conceptions of community and church – involuntarily led them in the direction of their own destruction. As Harry Pross, a sympathetic but cool-headed advocate of youth movements, has observed: 'In none of the great social groups from which it drew its recruits was the youth movement able to find a foothold against the seductions of National Socialism. Middle-class homes, the churches, schools for the most part indoctrinated with nationalistic thought – none of these had any arguments to offer against the events of Spring 1933.'

Cold figures reveal to what extent the churches missed their chance of shielding vulnerable young people from seduction and educating them into free, independent and mentally and spiritually alert human beings.

In 1928 Catholic Youth of Germany (*Katholische Jugend Deutschlands*), the root organisation of all Catholic youth clubs and societies, had a membership of 1,700,000. A select society such as *Neu-deutschland* (which set out to produce 'complete human beings' in a unity of life and religion) comprised about 2,500 young people in 1930.

In that same year there were about six hundred thousand young people in the Protestant organisations. While the Catholic organisations were based on congregations (first introduced by the Jesuits at the time of the religious wars), the Protestant groups tended to operate outside the church, taking their cue from the Anglo-Saxon world, which placed the accent on Christian deeds rather than beliefs. The German *Christlicher Verein Junger Männer*, established in 1883, was part of the World Alliance of Young Men's Christian Associations, set up in 1855. A federation of free church youth organisations, dating from 1903, included, among other (mainly Anglo-Saxon) youth groups, the Young People's Society of Christian Endeavour, founded in America by Dr Francis E. Clark, of which there was also a branch in Germany.

In the period 1918 to 1933 the development of German Protestant youth organisations was considerably influenced by mental attitudes arising out of the First World War. The Protestants had identified themselves body and soul with the German cause, and they regarded Germany's defeat in 1918 as a personal catastrophe. Leaders of the various organisations for young women as well as for young men tended after 1920 to be conservative in their approach to both church and national affairs. A more progressive and realistic outlook was discernible in the *Bund deutscher Jugendvereine* (Federation of German Youth Organisations) which, under the leadership of Wilhelm Stählin, tried to promote understanding of democracy, the parliamentary system and the workers' movement. Hermann Schafft's *Neuwerk Jugend* occupied a special place. Under the influence of Karl Barth, Paul Tillich (who was later to become a leading theologian in the United States) and two other creative personalities who also emigrated to America, Eugen Rosenstock-Huessy and Eduard Heimann, this

Adolf Kolping,
1813–65, founder
of Roman Catholic
youth organizations.

group explored relationships with working-class youth and experimented with colonies dedicated to the preservation of human beings and their natural surroundings.

The left-wing elements of the German Protestant youth movement, though few in number, experienced a remarkable renaissance in the Federal Republic after the Second World War. Rudi Dutschke was only one of a number of left-wing student leaders to emanate from Protestant student communities. A similar development can be detected among the Catholics: a number of student communities have broken away from the orthodox church-led youth organisations, which – both Protestant and Catholic – are now deeply engaged in trying to find their own identity among the general uncertainties of our present world.

The German youth movement, 1897-1933

The German youth movement began in Berlin in the summer of 1896 with a schoolboys' rambling club and ended at Whitsun 1933 with the last meeting of the free association of youth clubs in Munsterlager. After that the *Hitler-Jugend* (Hitler Youth) took over and destroyed it.

In 1913 the youth movement had about sixty thousand members; in 1927 over four million, in ninety-six separate organisations. It remains to this day the largest voluntary organisation of young people ever to have grown up from below, as distinct from being imposed from above.

It owed its existence less to the religious youth organisations that had preceded it than to the example set by women in their struggle for emancipation. The first women's organisations in Germany had been founded in 1860 to fight against male domination in the family and for educational equality and the right of entry to the universities. Working-class women in particular suffered under male domination. Factory-owners looked on them as easy game. Their husbands, returning drunk in the evenings, worked off their weakness and despair by behaving as domestic tyrants. The rising of sons against fathers in Germany followed that of women against men. As Harry Pross has remarked, many German sons at the turn of the century had revolutionary, freedom-loving mothers and conservative fathers striving anxiously to keep things as they were.

The German empire, whose stability had been regarded with profound misgiving by its founder Bismarck from the very beginning of 1871, was based on the idea of male dominance under the rule of virile leaders. The weak and unstable emperor Wilhelm II, though gifted, was undisciplined and ill-trained. He attempted to disguise both his weaknesses of character and his physical deformity under the mantle of a royal and ruler-like manner. He was the superman in uniform, and in his state the military officer occupied the first place. A socially ambitious industrialist or professor from the middle classes expected his son to be – at the very least – an officer of the reserve; while for his daughter only a military officer or a young nobleman would do for a husband. Male dictatorship was everywhere; in the factory bosses like Krupp in the Ruhr district, in the coal barons of Silesia, in the junkers of East Prussia with their power of life and death over their peasants and their itinerant Polish labourers. Civil servants, judges, professors, teachers: their male rule was absolute. The schoolmaster was a non-commissioned officer in civilian clothes, the professor a general. Like a pope he

A soldier's play, *The Emperor's Youngest Guardsman*, **left**, turns to bitter reality in 1914: on 1 August the German emperor orders general mobilization throughout Germany, **opposite**.

headed the absolute church of German learning, protecting pure knowledge against the attacks of heretics, outsiders and political nonconformists. Schoolchildren, students, apprentices, sons – these were just so much human material, to be used as the state thought fit. In 1865 special artillery manoeuvres for young people were held in Frankfurt. Young boys manned the guns and gave the order to fire. The march on Paris could begin. . . . For true German youngsters in the time of Kaiser Wilhelm it was the height of bliss to wear a sailorsuit. Young naval cadets in Berlin were much envied their opportunity to play with the Kaiser's favourite toy in Grunewald, a huge model warship, and thus prepare themselves to sail against England. . . .

The beginnings of the German youth movement

were non-political. It was a flight from the town into the country and its forests. Its centre was the camp-fire, its form of expression folk-singing and folk-dancing. There were strong feelings against capitalism and industrialisation. Karl Fischer, the leader of the *Wandervogel* (Ramblers) in Berlin-Steglitz, made no secret of his desire for youth reform on a national basis, and this pan-German feeling continued to influence the youth leaders in one way or another right up to the movement's ignominious end in 1933.

The various organisations within the youth movement covered a wide spectrum of political and philosophical opinion. Men of very varying views came from their ranks, such as the extreme right-

wing writers Friedrich and Georg Jünger; Johannes R. Becher and Alfred Kurella (poets and ministers in the government of the German Democratic Republic); the National Socialist minister of education, Franz Rust; Höss, the commandant of Auschwitz; as well as men who took part in the German resistance movement in the years 1939–44 – a whole list of poets, writers, artists, educationalists and politicians from both right and left. As Professor Helmut Gollwitzer said at a meeting of the *Freideutsche Jugend* (Free German Youth) in 1963, the youth movement offered everything that could be found in the world of adults as well.

Professor Gollwitzer was speaking on the fiftieth anniversary of the meeting of the *Freideutsche*

The mass of ordinary people experienced the outbreak of the first world war in a kind of delirium.

Freideutscher
Jugendtag 1913
Jahrhundertfeier
auf dem Hohen Meißner
am 11.-12. Oktober

Announcement of a mass rally to commemorate the centenary of Napoleon's defeat.

Below:
On the eve of the outbreak of World War 1 the German youth movement reached its culminating point.

Jugend, which took place on the Hoher Meissner mountain in 1913. At this first great representative gathering the motto was coined: 'Free German youth will shape its life in its own way, on its own responsibility and with inner conviction.'

Was that just an empty phrase?

Friedrich Nietzsche had once made a plea for an 'empire of youth'. Early leaders of the youth movement had been inspired by the myth of the New Man. Gustav Wyneken has seen in this the possible beginnings of a youth culture (or, as we would say today, a counter-culture). And certainly in their uniforms, their walking clothes, their hair styles, their private languages, their ceremonies, pointers to the counter-culture of today can be seen. It has been said of the German youth movement: 'Its spiritual life was one single dialogue.' This too smacks of the future.

On their ramblings the young people developed a new attitude towards life, which gradually spread

out to infect people of German origin living in
Poland and Czechoslovakia. Young people in
Rumania, France, Italy and Britain were also
influenced. In the last years of the Weimar Republic
the new attitude began to take practical forms.
Living communities and 'free' schools were set up
in country districts. (Many aspects of the German
school reform movement owed their origin to the
German youth movement.) Nature conservancy
was always a strong point, both at home and abroad.
Rolf Gardiner, an English member of the international youth movement between the years
1923–33, was encouraged by German friends to
found a colony, Springhead, at Fontmell Magna,
near Shaftesbury. The British-American Biodynamic Association, which in the period 1933–45
campaigned actively against the pollution of our
natural resources, maintained a close contact with
former members of the German youth movement.
Mother Earth, the journal of the Soil Association,
continued in the post-war period to propagate the
ideas of this movement, with which a surprisingly
large number of present experts in the field of
nature conservation in Germany were formerly
associated.

Concern for the problems of an industrial society
was a much later development. In 1927, under the
sponsorship of Graf Moltke, a study group was set
up in Kreisau, and a plan was worked out for the
first labour camps. (Kreisau became in the war
years a centre of the resistance against Hitler, and,
following the failure of the assassination attempt in
July 1944, Graf Moltke was executed.)

There were distinct signs that the German youth
movement was facing both ways, particularly in the
realm of politics and in its attitude towards sex. In
politics several of the component groups sought to
grasp the opportunity of putting into practice their
new spirit of fraternity by living, like the early
Christians, in close communities. They set up rural
communes, in which there were no leaders and no
followers. The relationship of leader to follower in
the German youth movement bore no resemblance

Overleaf: Groups of
youths called
Wandervogel, into
which girls were
admitted for the first
time, now gained new
impetus and grew in
popularity.

to the insidious form which later developed in the *Hitler Jugend*, which demanded from its members unquestioning obedience to the will of the leader. Such unconditional obedience was unknown in the German youth movement. The members' attitude to their chosen leaders was based on confidence and respect, which could always be withdrawn. Evidence of this inner freedom can be seen in the large number of allied and opposed groups into which the youth movement eventually split.

As to its sexual attitudes, the *Wandervogel* club, with which the German youth movement began, was to start with exclusively male membership. Girls were eventually permitted to join, but with considerable reluctance. There was without doubt a tinge of homosexuality among some of the early leaders of the movement, and in any case there is an ingrained tendency in the German character to despise the female sex. Other branches of the youth movement moved in the direction of nudism. A magazine entitled *Die Schönheit* (Beauty) was started in Berlin in 1904. In one issue of this

Youth movements spanned a wide spectrum: from Jewish groups to groups inspired by a new 'Germanic Paganism' and groups devoted to open-air nudism.

magazine in the year 1906 Professor G. Hermann, a
man well known in *Wandervogel* circles, proclaimed
what he called 'Nudo-Natio', a movement in
defence of 'God's noble gift of nakedness'. The
professor wrote: 'Since in this prudish Europe of
ours a nudist organisation can hardly hope for legal
recognition, my friends have drawn up a proclamation addressed to all who are no longer prepared to
deny the nakedness of their birth and their identity
with Nudo-Natio. It is proposed that the Prince of
Monaco should be asked to grant us permission to
establish a colony there.' The Prince turned them
down.

In its failure to find a genuine new basis for the
relationship between the sexes Elisabeth Busse
Wilson sees a reason for the complete failure of the
German youth movement. Too many inhibitions
remained unsolved. The many early marriages in
Wandervogel circles often broke down – partly
because neither the girls not the boys were mature
enough in their attitudes to sex, and partly because
only very few of the youth movement leaders were
even interested in the subject of sexual education.

An advertisement in the magazine *Der Wandervogel* in the year 1917 offered its female readers
'new Germanic trinkets', among them a brooch
consisting of a sword between two swastikas. The
ancient Germanic idea was one that haunted several
different groups within the youth movement. A
vague and diffuse sort of nature worship, combined
with resentment against the established church,
paved the way for a later infiltration by National
Socialist elements. After 1918 there arose a Catholic
youth movement which adopted Romano Guardini
as its spiritual leader. Among the older politicians,
scientists and journalists at present active in the
German Federal Republic, not a few come from the
ranks of the former Catholic and Protestant youth
movements.

The sociological basis of the German youth
movement was from its very beginning a narrow
one. The vast majority of its members came from a
middle-class background, their parents being

The early days of the Wandervogel. Karl Fischer, one of the founder members, is third from the right. This picture was taken at Easter, 1898.

mainly teachers and civil servants. There were very few from the working class, from the aristocracy or the world of rich industrialists. It was a movement that reflected the fears of a young middle-class generation that saw its identity threatened by the rising of the new 'masses'. In this respect it showed a definite affinity with the middle classes, which in Germany had slipped down in the social scale since 1918, and with the lower middle classes, both of which were terrified of being swallowed up by the 'red flood' – and in consequence voted Hitler into power.

Following the Second World War the *Wandervogel* idea experienced a rebirth in France. After the liberation of their country from German occupation in 1945, young French people took to wandering through the countryside in singing groups. Like their German predecessors, they were mostly students and schoolchildren from middle-class families. Even in the war years, in the period 1940–45, there had been strong intellectual contacts with the German spirit among the French underground. Sartre and Merleau-Ponty had discovered Heidegger and Hegel, and subsequently the young Karl Marx, even before 1940. The early surrealists had introduced Hölderlin and Novalis to Paris back in the Twenties. Now it was the turn of Nietzsche and (as in 1830) the German Romantics to influence young Frenchmen.

But the country in which the ideals of the German youth movement have found their clearest expression is Israel. They can be seen, in a modified from, in the *kibbutz*, where men live free on their own free land. The German Jewish youth movement *Blau-Weiss* (Blue and White) started in Berlin and Breslau in 1907. Five years later the Jewish *Wanderbund* was founded, and its songs and campfires reveal the influence of the German youth movement. In March 1918 preparations for the move to Palestine began to be made. Farming schools for young people were set up in 1923 in various parts of Germany. The last meeting of the *Blau-Weiss* movement took place in Dresden in 1925.

Title page of the *Eisbrecher* (the Icebreaker), a leading paper of the German youth movement.

The German youth movement came to grief because none of its component groups had a clear conception of the nature and obligations of power. It was unable to formulate its political aims, long-term or short-term. Its picture of a new society was vague, so that in practical terms it could be said to have had none.

National Socialism came to fill this political vacuum. Most of the groups inside the youth movement did not want it. Now at last they strove to come to terms, intellectually and emotionally, with the Weimar Republic, with the ideas of democracy and the realities of the technical revolution. But they were too late.

Young revolutionaries in eastern Europe

Russia

The nineteenth century saw the beginnings of underground movements in tsarist Russia. Their members were mainly young aristocrats, military officers, students and writers. In origin these were the sons of the middle-range aristocracy, the higher and middle reaches of the civil service, the lower middle class and – not to be forgotten – the priesthood of the Eastern Orthodox Church. Lenin and Trotsky were typical (if, in their personalities, exceptional) products of these nineteenth century Russian youth movements.

The starting point of the First World War in 1914 was the assassination of the heir to the Austrian throne, the Archduke Franz Ferdinand. All of the six assassins were less than twenty years old, and they came from secret societies of schoolchildren and students, which in the Balkans – as in Russia – made world history.

Up to the middle of the nineteenth century there were only two social classes in Russia: the aristocrats and the peasants. The aristocrats held almost all the country's wealth in their hands, had a monopoly of all social privileges and dominated Russia's intellectual life. The remaining ninety per cent of the Russian population belonged to the peasant class. Almost entirely illiterate, the majority of them were totally dependent on their masters who thought nothing of now and again staking hundreds or thousands of 'souls', as these peasants were called, on a game of cards. These masses were kept in order by a military autocracy, ruling with the help of an army of bureaucrats and a police force recruited from Baltic Germans. Ruling meant maintaining law and order within the country and waging wars outside it. In the second half of the eighteenth century the lands of the tsar had been shaken by a large-scale peasants' revolt under the leadership of

In Russia the masses were completely at the mercy of their lords and masters. **Left**: a caricature by Dore; **below**: Cossacks drive the demonstrators of 5 January 1905 from St Petersburg's Palace Square.

Pugachëv. Joseph de Maistre, who knew Russia well and had a deep loathing for the Eastern Orthodox Church, remarked at the beginning of the nineteenth century that the great danger for the Russian regime would lie eventually not in the peasants, but in a 'university Pugachëv'. And throughout the nineteenth century the tsars themselves were highly suspicious of their schools and universities.

'Russians, awake!' cried Alexander Labtsin, who died in exile in 1825. This was Russia's year of fate,

The Polish poet Adam Mickiewicz, **above**, and Russian poet Michael Yuryewitch Lermontov, **below**, belonged to the intellectual leadership in the struggle against Tsarist oppression.

equivalent to the year 1848 in other European countries. Tsar Alexander I, who had previously been hailed by the young generation in Russia and the rest of Europe as a great future hope, had become a reactionary by 1815. He handed the reins of power over to his war minister, General Arakcheyev, whose secret ambition, it was murmured, was to turn the whole country into a parade ground for blindly obedient soldiers. Taking their model from a secret society of patriotic German students, the *Tugendbund* (League of Virtue), young Russian officers, aristocrats and students set up a number of revolutionary cells. The Rescue League of 1816 developed into the illegal Welfare League of 1818. This in turn split up into the Northern League, to which the poet Rydeyev and Pushkin's friends Küchelbecker and Delvig belonged, and the Southern League. In 1823 two literary circles were established in Moscow (and disbanded two years later). One, led by S. Raitch, was the Literary Society, the other the Society for Devotees of Wisdom. The president of the latter was the twenty-year-old Prince Vladimir Odoyevsky, its secretary an eighteen-year-old named Fenevitinov, a product of German Romanticism who was interested in founding an autonomous Russian system of philosophy. Through this (he believed) Russia would gain its moral freedom, as a preliminary to political freedom.

In 1825 occurred the Decembrist rising, instigated by aristocratic young officers and intellectuals who hoped to reform the state from within along the lines of west European Enlightenment. This revolt, which had no contacts with the people, took place on the death of Alexander I. It was put down. Forty of the revolutionaries were condemned to death (though only five were executed), and more than eighty sent to Siberia. Only women clung heroically to their support, forerunners of the many politically and intellectually dedicated young Russian women without whom none of the illegal underground movements in Russia up to 1917 would have been even conceivable.

Russia relapsed into a deathlike stillness. Alexander's successor, Tsar Nicholas I, known as 'the crowned policeman', grew steadily more terrified as the years went by. In the final years of his reign he had even the chairs of philosophy at the universities abolished.

'A dog's death for a dog', wrote the Tsar on the military report of the death of Lermontov, who died in prison in 1841 at the age of twenty-seven. At the age of sixteen Mikhail Yuryevich Lermontov had written his 'Prophecy': 'The year will come, a black year for Russia, when the Tsar's crown will fall. The people will forget its previous love for the crown, and the food for many will be death and blood.' In 1839 he wrote in 'Meditation': 'I look on our generation with concern. Its future is either empty or dark.'

Lermontov was a friend of the Polish poet Mickiewicz (whose work he translated into Russian) and other Poles in St Petersburg. An awakening young generation of Russians and Poles met together there in a secret society called The Sixteen. Their guiding star was Byron.

Lermontov, a descendant of both Russian and Scottish aristocracy (he claimed descent from the eleventh century Scottish chieftain Learmont), prophesied the collapse of the aristocratic regime. 'But you, arrogant successors of ancestors well known for their depravity. . . .'

Discontented young aristocrats abandoned their state service to enter universities or travel abroad. They went to Paris and to Berlin – and among them was Bakunin, the most revolutionary of all European thinkers in the nineteenth century and one whose anarchic influence long outlived him. He was the inspiration for revolutionary youth in France, Italy and the Balkans; above all in Catalonia on the eve of the Spanish civil war of 1936; and later, during our own time, in both Americas as well as in Europe.

Mikhail Bakunin (1814–76) fought actively on all revolutionary fronts, intellectual as well as political. He was in Berlin in 1840 and again from 1844 to

Leon Trotsky at eighteen. He gave his photograph to Alexandra Lvovna with the dedication: 'Circumstances may alter and living-conditions change . . . but you must never change!'

1847. From 1848 onwards he was a hunted man. Twice he was condemned to death. In 1851 he was captured and handed over to the Russians. After years of imprisonment he was sent to permanent exile in Siberia. He escaped in 1861 and went to Japan, then to America and Britain. He died in Berne in 1876.

Bakunin saw revolution as a matter for the free individual. He was against totalitarian revolutions and for this reason earned little love from Marx or Stalin, though Lenin owed more to him than he would admit. It is this aspect that makes him attractive to youthful revolutionaries, who are constantly nagged by the fear that every revolution may turn into a reactionary counter-revolution, bringing merely new jailers, new tsars, new demands for conformity.

In 1847 Bakunin wrote to Herwegh from Paris: 'We can be happy only when the whole globe is in flames.' To his Polish friend Storzkowsky he said: 'I seek God in men, in their love, in their freedom. And now I am seeking God in revolution.' Bakunin saw the state as an altar on which priests of a political religion sacrificed the true community of men. The state was twin to the church. It was Moloch, living on human sacrifices. In a famous speech delivered in Geneva in 1867 before an audience said to have included Dostoevsky, Bakunin spoke of a coming world war in which all states would destroy each other nationally, politically and culturally. Powerful states, he said, can protect themselves only by criminal means.

Much of Bakunin's thinking still seems startlingly modern. Banished to Siberia, he very soon found his feet. His cousin Muravëv-Amursky, who was governor-general there, had gathered around him in Irkutsk a number of young intellectuals, all recruited from among the exiles. It was Muravëv-Amursky who had conquered the Amur territory (hence his honorary name Amursky) and extended the Russian empire to the Pacific Ocean. Here, from his Siberian stronghold, Muravëv planned to modernise and reform the tsar's empire – building a New Russia on virgin soil on the lines of the United States of America.

In European Russia the main revolutionary school was the university. Here young aristocrats who had escaped from the tsar and their families came together with young people of a lower social order and with the *rasnochintsi*, young men who – as private tutors, translators and provincial journalists – had laboriously worked their way up from the social misery and poverty of their origins.

This was the beginning of the so-called Russian 'intelligentsia'. The word itself was coined in about 1860, when the *rasnochintsi* began to assume control of the movement, which was both intellectual and political. In this period of social change the conflict between 'fathers' and 'sons' can be seen at work. The fathers were philosophical idealists, romanticists and aesthetes. The sons attempted to realise their fathers' ideals of freedom, humanity, reason and democracy – by revolutionary means.

A pamphlet addressed to young people in 1861 proclaimed: 'We are a retarded nation, and that is our salvation. We must be thankful that we do not need to experience the life that is being lived in Europe.' (Similar tones have been heard among youth movements since 1945: in Africa, the Arab countries – and also among young blacks in the United States.) Another pamphlet, entitled 'Young Russia', proclaimed in 1862: 'From below can be heard the muffled grumbling of a people plundered and oppressed by anybody who holds even a small amount of power in his hands. . . . Over them stands a small heap of happy and contented people with the tsar at their head. . . . The only escape from this terrible situation is through revolution – a pitiless, bloody revolution which will completely and fundamentally change the existing social order and destroy its present supporters. We are not afraid, although we know that streams of blood will be shed and many innocent victims will perhaps lose their lives.'

In 1840 there were roughly three thousand university students in the tsar's empire, which had a

F

Russia's universities of the nineteenth century were fertile ground for revolutionary ideas. Under the leadership of young students of 'noble families' resistance aginst the Tsarist regime grew: **left** trial of the Czar's assassins; St Petersburg, 1881: **below** execution of Nihilists: **below left** arrest of 400 Moscow students in 1881. The youthful Lenin, **right**, was greatly affected by these events.

population of over forty million. More than ninety per cent of the people were illiterate. In 1860 there were 4,500 students, and in 1870, by which time the total population had risen to more than seventy-five million, students numbered a little over five thousand. The government's hand lay heavily on all schools and universities. It is surprising how many of the Russian intelligentsia, from Belinsky and Herzen to Lenin, Trotsky and Stalin, were expelled or suspended from school. After that there were further obstacles to overcome in the shape of censorship, the suppression of periodicals or perhaps arrest, if too much was said in print. These young intellectuals, forced to exchange critical thinking for revolutionary action, consisted mainly of disciplined students and censored journalists, driven by despair into conspiracy.

By 1890 censorship was at the height of severity, schools were available only to children of wealthy parents, universities had lost their independence and higher education courses for women (who were not admitted to the universities) had been abolished. From this time onwards young women, students and senior schoolchildren formed the nucleus of the revolutionary movement. In 1896 students were called on to swear an oath of allegiance to the new Tsar, Nicholas ii. Most of the students in St Petersburg, Moscow and Kiev refused. Many of them preferred to emigrate or to vanish underground.

'Teeth clenched, Vladimir sat through his final school examinations. There still exists a photograph of him taken at that time, obviously for his school-leaving certificate. Over the still unformed, yet very concentrated face with its overlip pushed defiantly forward, there lies a shadow of suffering and deep hatred. Two deaths stood at the beginning of this new period in Vladimir's life. That of his father, in the natural process of age, awoke in him a critical attitude towards the church and the myth of religion. The execution of his brother aroused a glowing hatred for the executioners.'

Thus wrote Trotsky about Lenin the schoolboy.

The execution of Lenin's adored elder brother Alexander (Sasha) mobilised powers that were to shake the world to its foundations. Sasha had entered the preparatory class of his high school in 1874. 'Notwithstanding the previous epoch of reforms the high school was at that time a sort of penal establishment for the improvement of young boys. As the creators of the teaching system explained: "The study of ancient languages teaches humility through the very difficulty of achieving success, and humility is the first mark and the first requirement of true education." Classicism was called on to play the role of an iron yoke into which the childish understanding had to be forced. Church attendance was strictly regulated, and it made a misery of the holidays.'

Trotsky is drawing here on his own experience. 'Permanent strained relations led in many high schools to violent explosions and even to conspiracies against teachers who were particularly hated.' *Hatred of school became a sort of national tradition.* The poet Nadson, who belonged to the same generation as Sasha, wrote of his school days: 'A curse on my school and boyhood years, which

Cossacks in street fighting, St Petersburg, 1905.

were without love, friendship, freedom. . .'

Trotsky relates: 'More than most of his fellow scholars, Alexander found the harshness and cruelty of the school regime hard to bear. But he clenched his teeth and studied on. . . . On 1 March 1881, when Alexander was in the sixth class, a momentous piece of news was received from St Petersburg: the Tsar had been killed by revolutionaries. The whole town seethed with rumours and suspicion. The school director Kerensky made a speech about the crime committed against the liberator tsar. The teacher of religion described the death of the divinely anointed monarch as a martyr's death and branded the revolutionaries as "the dregs of humanity".'

It was in memory of 1 March 1881 that six young men made an attempt on 1 March 1887 to assassinate Tsar Alexander III. Only one of them was as old as twenty-six; the others were all between twenty and twenty-one. Alexander Ulyanov took all the blame on himself. On the manifesto prepared by Alexander Ulyanov, then twenty-one, the thirty-two-year-old Tsar Alexander Romanov wrote: 'This is not simply the work of a madman, but of a complete idiot.' Against the assertion in the manifesto that under the prevailing system of government it was almost impossible to work for a rise in the living standards of the people, the Tsar wrote: 'That is a comfort.' The manifesto called for a democratic system and demanded the nationalisation of farms, factories and all means of production. Against this the Tsar noted: 'Pure communism.'

Five of the accused were hanged. The plot, it appeared, had been confined to a small group of students. There had been no attempt to spread propaganda, no approach to the workers, no printing press, no periodical. The conspirators had not reckoned on support, either from the liberals or from the people.

Vladimir Ulyanov resolved to avenge the brother he both loved and respected, but to do things better than that romantic young idealist had set out to do on his own. The revolution would first be prepared on paper in a long process of argument and propaganda. The revolt itself would be carried out by a hard core of professional revolutionaries. (In his own way Lenin 'ignored' the people exactly as his brother Alexander had done.) Trotsky later wrote that Lenin's personal character, his ideas and his methods of putting them into practice were all formed between the ages of seventeen and twenty-three.

Young scholars abandoned the tsarist schools and universities to enter the hard school of revolution, and with it to stand or fall. It was from the ranks of these individualists of a red youth movement that many victims of the abortive Soviet Revolution came. After the death of Lenin in 1924 they succumbed to the autocratic Stalin and his bureaucracy. Trotsky writes in his autobiography of the unleashing of the *petit bourgeois* in the Bolshevist soul. Party bureaucrats of this new kind accused Trotsky himself of being an individualist and an aristocrat. 'Over a bottle of wine or going home after a visit to the ballet one self-satisfied bureaucrat would say to another: "All he can think of is his permanent revolution".'

In Trotsky's conception of permanent revolution one can see many ideas combined. There is the old, prophetic Jewish sense of mission, and there is also an element of anarchy, such as Bakunin, that unseen and unacknowledged spiritual father of the young Lenin, had put forward to the youth of the world as a future goal.

For the revolutionary youth of Russia the main target was a social one, though there are traces of a messianic sort of nationalism to be seen – for example in the works of its greatest literary exponent, Dostoevsky. But for the oppressed Slav peoples revolution was first and foremost a nationalistic matter. As we have already seen, there were cross-connections between young Poles and young Russians: Mickiewicz and other young Poles were members of a secret society in St Petersburg. Pan-Slavism brought in its train the vision of a Slav brotherhood. A new generation of young people

would rise up together against their foreign overlords, the Emperor in Vienna, the Tsar in St
Petersburg (who was of German extraction anyway)
and the Turkish Sultan, who occupied Bosnia,
Hercegovina and Bulgaria in the Balkans. And not
only against them, but also against their own
feudalistic masters who were treacherously working
with the occupying powers.

Poland

The connections between the young Polish
nationalists and the restless young people of Russia
were, however, constantly being broken off, for
Poland and Russia shared with Germany the role
of arch-enemy. It had twice been partitioned
between Russia, Prussia and Austria (and was later
to be divided for a third time between Stalin and
Hitler). Throughout the nineteenth century there
was an underground movement of young Poles
ready to rise up against the Russian regime at a
sign from the West. The French revolt in 1830 and
after that the rising in 1848 were accepted as such
signals. But in both cases the Polish rebellions were
brutally put down.

Cossacks preventing
people from
approaching the
square in front of the
Winter Palace,
St Petersburg, during
the 1905 disturb-
ances.

In the nineteenth and twentieth centuries Polish freedom fighters frequently formed Polish legions, which fought in many European wars and also in America. Polish military cemeteries in the Libyan desert, in Monte Cassino and in Normandy bear witness to the undefeated will for freedom of a nation whose young people, headed by schoolchildren and students, had been gathering underground since the early years of the nineteenth century.

What these young people owed to their great national poets is not sufficiently recognised in the western world. As Elias Siberski has pointed out, the main body of Polish poetry arose directly out of the conspiratorial freedom movement, and in the century ending with the First World War it was for several successive generations a textbook for both conspiracy and socialism. Polish poetry is dominated by the three great romantic nationalists: Mickiewicz, Slowacki and Krasinski.

Konrad Wallenrod, by Adam Mickiewicz (1798–1855), was an urgent appeal to the Polish people to rise up against their Russian oppressors. In his drama *Dziady* (The Funeral) Mickiewicz summoned up the great spirits of Poland's past to rouse the people to the struggle for freedom. It was an attempt to suppress a performance of this drama that led in 1956 to the disturbances inside Poland against Russia and the country's own Stalinistic regime. Schoolchildren and students rose in revolt. The 'Polish October', as it was called, led straight to the rebellion in Hungary, when students and intellectuals gathered in their Petöfi clubs.

Among the pupils of Poland's secondary schools Mickiewicz's great epic poem *Pan Tadeusz* (1834) was the national bible. Witness for that is Marya Sklodowska, who later as Madame Curie became famous for her part in the discovery of radium. She speaks in her reminiscences of her enthusiasm for *Pan Tadeusz* when she was a pupil of the Lyceum of Warsaw. This school, staffed by Russian teachers and inspectors, lived in a state of cold war. The Polish schoolgirls hated their Russian teachers.

Demonstrators in
St Petersburg, 1905.

When the daughter of the Russian headmaster fell
ill with typhoid, pupils in the second class read a
mass in the hope that she would die. Infected by
their parents' terror of the Russian secret police,
the children lived in constant dread of deportation
to Siberia. Herr Homberg, German-Russian inspec-
tor of private schools in Warsaw, set a test for
Marya: to recite the names of the Russian tsars.
Fräulein Mayer, the hated supervisor of the Russian
institute to which Marya was finally sent, once

surprised two young Polish girls performing a dance
of joy over the assassination of Tsar Alexander II.

In the areas dominated by the Habsburg monarchy the school was a breeding ground of discontent against conservative fathers, teachers and the
government of Emperor Franz Joseph. The teachers
were themselves split. Some of them were conservative; others, however, had nationalist feelings of
their own and took a hand in guiding their pupils'
rebelliousness.

Typical of these schools was the *Realschule* in Linz, where Adolf Hitler was a pupil up to his fourteenth year. Though his reasons for leaving were not political, it was here, in an atmosphere of hatred and scorn for monarchist professors and imperial pomp in Vienna, that Hitler formed his first political ideas. As his conversation showed, he never forgot his school days in Linz.

Schoolchildren of all sorts, star pupils as well as those who were expelled, belonged to the many secret societies in which acts of rebellion were planned, culminating in the assassination of Archduke Franz Ferdinand at Sarajevo in 1914. When the young Hitler heard the news, he thought at first that students of German blood had killed the hated heir to the Austrian throne. Hitler, along with many other young people in the German-speaking part of the empire, was possessed with longing for a return to the German fatherland.

The pull of ancient blood ties was felt by many young Balkan rebels as they awoke to a sense of their country's historic identity. They evoked a mythical super-father to replace their own weak fathers, who were making common cause with the Habsburg monarchy. While German nationalists in Vienna, Linz and Innsbruck were calling on Wotan, young Bosnians and Slovenes were summoning the god Perun, the chief god of the Slav peoples, to their aid. A prose poem bearing the title 'The Mighty God Perun is among us' appeared on 1 January 1913 in the newspaper *Preporod*. 'We hear that you too are locked in battle,' it said. 'We hear the echoing voice of the god Perun. Friends, have courage! Do not yield, for we, the men of the Bosnian mountains, are with you heart and soul, and Perun is among us too, with his thunderous, all-conquering voice! Forward in the great battle for Yugoslavia!'

Yugoslavia

Yugoslavia – the country of the southern Slavs: that was the goal of which these young Slovenes, Croats and Bosnians dreamed in their search for a Balkan fatherland. They established contacts with young Germans, and even stronger ones with young

Russians. The first meeting between young Bosnians and Slovenes took place in Vienna in the university term 1910–11. Gačinovič, the leader of the Young Bosnians, gave Fabjančič, the leader of the Young Slovenes, a Russian handbook on the subject of organising secret societies based on cells and a central headquarters. Another gift from Gačinovič to his Slovene blood-brothers consisted of four pamphlets by Bakunin.

Gavrilo Princip, Franz Ferdinand's assassin, was born into a family of serfs in the Grahovo valley of West Bosnia, a blood-soaked territory over which the church of Rome and the church of Byzantium had fought for a thousand years. The peasant population had finally been enslaved by the Turks. Writing of the peasants' revolt in 1875 against their Turkish overlords in Hercegovina, Sir Arthur Evans describes some of the brutalities to which the Bosnian peasants were subjected. During the hot summers men would be stripped naked and tied to trees, their bodies smeared with honey. There they were left to the mercies of the insects. In the winters there were easier forms of torture. People were simply bound to stakes barefoot and left to stand there until their feet froze.

Gavrilo Princip's family had provided three successive generations of rebels. After the unsuccessful rising of 1875 the women and children of the family crossed the border and sought asylum in Austria. There they were housed in refugee camps, a habitual source of irritation and embitterment, as recent events in Algeria and Jordan remind us.

Religion was a constant cause of internal trouble in Bosnia. At school Catholic, Orthodox and Moslem children were taught to hate one another, and for many of them this was the only lesson they ever learned and remembered in adult life. During the Second World War Roman Catholic Croat bands led by Franciscans wiped out something between six hundred and eight hundred thousand Serbs of the Orthodox faith – men, women and children.

While still at high school Gavrilo Princip

dreamed of becoming a poet. (At the same time Hitler was in Vienna, dreaming of becoming a painter.) The year 1911, when he was in the fifth class of the high school at Sarajevo, was a fateful one for him: he began to take a passionate interest in political ideals. In February of the following year he was expelled from school for having taken part in demonstrations against the Sarajevo authorities. Austria had annexed Bosnia-Hercegovina in 1908. Princip journeyed on foot to Belgrade and, as he crossed the border, threw himself down to kiss the soil of Serbia. He had returned to his fatherland. 'In almost every family there was a revolt of the

young against the old generation', writes Vladimir Dedijer. 'This applied not only to Gavrilo Princip, but to many of the Young Bosnians.' It was a revolt against 'capitalistic' fathers. Gavrilo Princip, on the eve of the assassination in Sarajevo, directed his hatred against the *čaršija*, the business quarter of the town. 'If I could force the whole *čaršija* into a matchbox,' he said, 'I should set it alight.' Gaćinović expressed his disgust with the older generation in this way: 'Our fathers, our dictators are true tyrants, who drag us along with them and try to make us do what *they* want with our lives.' While Gavrilo was making preparations for the

In 1905 the sailors on board the battleship *Potemkin* mutinied. **Below**: funeral of the victims; **below left**: the leader of the mutineers, Matsuchenko, (in white shirt) after surrender.

assassination, his father was hoisting a black and yellow flag, the symbol of loyalty, in front of his house to greet the Austrian heir to the throne on his visit to Sarajevo. The political murder of a representative figure of the enemy state had overtones of ordinary patricide. In this connection it is interesting to note that young Bosnians who remained at home in the shadow of their own fathers were in favour of political assassination, whereas older members of the young generation – or at any rate those who had escaped from home to study abroad – disapproved of the murder of Franz Ferdinand.

The assassination of the Austrian heir was a culmination of events, rather than an isolated event in itself. Schools in Slovenia, Croatia and Bosnia were in a state of permanent strike against the Habsburg school system, which was attempting to make good Austrians and good Catholics out of these Slav children. Groups of schoolchildren and groups of students were all busy preparing acts of rebellion. In 1910 Emperor Franz Joseph came near to being assassinated at the same spot on which in 1914 Franz Ferdinand fell. The great school strike of March 1912 in Dalmatia was prepared by secret societies of the schoolchildren themselves. In Sarajevo Gavrilo Princip went from class to class, threatening punishment to all pupils unwilling to join in demonstrations.

In March 1912 there were between five and six thousand schoolchildren on strike in Zagreb alone. They greeted the assassination of the governor, Count Cuvaj, on 8 June 1912 with enthusiasm. The chief assassin, a student named Jukič, was twenty-five years old, but the eleven others brought to trial with him in August were schoolboys between the ages of fifteen and eighteen. One of them, the fifteen-year-old Djuka čvijić, reminded the court of the classic theory of tyrannicide: 'Jukić told me we should kill Cuvaj, for it is not a crime, but a good deed, to kill a tyrant.' When Jukić was sentenced to death a young girl sitting in the courtroom threw him a rose. In such very young people, love, puberty and erotic feeling are an integral part of their political emotions. In the journal of a secret society in Zadar, the capital city of Dalmatia, a poem was published on 14 August 1912 in honour of the twelve accused: 'Hail to the twelve apostles, to the glorious thoughts of the Nazarene! Hail to you, to whom we take off our hats and bow down to the dark earth.'

In this poem the new gospel of these young nationalists was proclaimed. 'The dawn is breaking. . . . From our necks the blood will spurt. . . . From blood will come freedom. Hail to you, L. J. !'

L. J. was Luka Jukić. As the leader writer of *Pester Lloyd* rightly pointed out after Sarajevo, 'Jukić's act was simply the dress rehearsal for Princip's gun-shots.' It was only after the school-children's demonstrations in Sarajevo that Princip decided to kill a high member of the Habsburg family; before that his victim might well have been some 'old man' from his own people.

The youngest of Princip's associates, Cvetko Popović, afterwards wrote: 'Since I was convinced I should live only until 28 June, I saw everything from a different angle. I forgot my schoolbooks.' Early in 1914 Princip was preparing for his sixth form school examinations. He was living in a dream world of poetic, erotic and political fantasies, immersing himself in the visions of his favourite poets Sima Pandurović ('Lament for a Dead Sweetheart', 'Loathing for the Emptiness of Life,' etc.) and Vladimir Vidrić. Princip copied out Pandurović's poem 'Our Today' (which first appeared in 1912) and underlined the following passage: 'Even if we ourselves have so far created nothing,/at least we should put an end to the miseries of our times./Our grave will be the foundation stone/for a new life, free of present errors,/for the better life that must lead somewhere:/if not to an honourable peace, then to war;/if not to happiness, at any rate to freedom.'

Princip was fond of quoting a poem by Nietzsche to which he was passionately devoted: 'Yes, I know whence I come!/Insatiable like a flame/I glow and burn away./All that I touch becomes light,/All that

Overleaf: Many students declared their solidarity with Potemkin's sailors: a student demonstration, St Petersburg, 18 October 1905.

I leave is ash./Certainly I am flame.'

If Princip had not committed the murder, there was another who would have done it – Ivan Endlicher, a young Slovene of German extraction. 'Should I be afraid of children?' asked Archduke Franz Ferdinand. He was fully aware of the unrest around him, but he had no patience with security measures. 'Wherever we are, we are in God's hand', he said. 'Caution and anxiety make life too difficult. Fear is always a dangerous business.' In 1913 Count Carlo Collas, head of the political section in the provincial government of Bosnia, wrote a report on the Young Bosnians, emphasising the tenseness of the situation. His action almost cost him his job – because he had shown himself to be 'afraid of children'.

But it can certainly be said that the assassination in Sarajevo, quite apart from its worldwide political implications, was a tragedy staged by children. Apparently the first to realise that were Franz Ferdinand's own young sons, who publicly forgave the young assassins. These young Bosnians had been carrying out a children's crusade – the counter-crusade of a group of young believers against the crusade of the Roman Catholic Church, which with the help of the Habsburgs (and above all Franz Ferdinand) was attempting to prise the Balkans away from the Eastern Church.

On 28 June 1914, immediately after hearing the news of Franz Ferdinand's death, a schoolboy, Todor Ilić, wrote in his diary: 'Murder is the greatest god of all, for it proves that Young Bosnia lives, that it possesses men who are prepared for martyrdom. The life of a race lies in its blood, blood is the nation's god, death takes the place of rebellion, and assassination is the mutiny of a nation.' It is a statement in which the ideas of Bakunin and other anarchists are mixed with an ardent racialist nationalism.

How did the children's tragedy end? Gavrilo Princip, mortally ill, dreamed away his life in the prison of Theresienstadt (later, between 1942 and 1945, this was to become the concentration camp hell of Terezin). He told a visiting psychiatrist, Martin Pappenheim: 'Mostly I sleep for only about four hours each night. I dream a lot – nice dreams about life and love, not at all frightening. . . . I was an idealistic person and wanted to avenge my people. My motives were revenge and love. . .'

In 1915 the Austrian poet Franz Werfel visited Princip's accomplice Čabrinović in Theresienstadt. 'He is twenty years old. . . . In these lost features I saw all the beauty and dignity of that unfathomable loneliness which emanates from a man who can never again live among human beings. . . . This youth was chosen to be a man of destiny. . . . Was it the murderers who committed murder? There stood this boy now, in the alien yellow light of his cell. . . . I still recall with surprise the beard surrounding Čabronović's suffering face, the sort of beard we associate with some of the saints of this earth.'

Franz Werfel saw this boy as an innocent lamb, a sacrificial lamb. On 23 January 1916 Čabronović died in Theresienstadt. On 28 April 1918 – as the First World War, in which millions of young men were herded to their deaths by the old men of the existing European order, was drawing to its close – Princip died in Theresienstadt of tuberculosis. In the first months of his captivity he had made his last attempt to write poetry, scribbling the following lines on the walls of his cell:

> Our ghosts prowl through Vienna and whisper
> in the palaces and make the masters tremble.

The 'masters' – the Emperor in Vienna, the Emperor in Berlin, the Tsar in St Petersburg, the Sultan in Constantinople, the princes and aristocrats of central and eastern Europe – were swept away by the First World War. But many old men remained. Theirs were the political acts that led straight to the Second World War. And it was with these aged representatives of the System (as the Establishment was called by young National Socialists) that the world's youth movements had to deal in the years after 1918.

Nie wieder Krieg

Mitteldeutscher Jugendtag
Leipzig 2.-4. August 1924

Youth as human material

In the years between the two world wars political power, both in Europe and America, was in the hands of men whose views had been formed in the years preceding the First World War and fixed by the war itself. Lacking in any sort of creative feeling or initiative, their policies were concerned more with consolidating the victory of 1918 than with thoughts of the future. They shared the failing of all conservative politicians, both now and then: young people interested them, not for their ideas, but simply for their potential value as party supporters and as soldiers in the next war – civil or otherwise.

In the control of young people Italy's fascist youth organisations provided the model, directly or indirectly, for all the states of Europe with leanings towards dictatorship. The most successful imitation was the *Hitler-Jugend* (Hitler Youth), the classical example of a youth organisation created from above. Not only did it manage to bring millions of young people under its control: it also succeeded in arousing their enthusiasm. These boys were prepared to face death for their beloved leader. Between the ages of eighteen and twenty-eight they fell on the battlefields, and among those who fell in the last fight in Berlin were fourteen-year-old boys. On 20 April 1945, his final birthday, Hitler decorated young boys with the Iron Cross. It was the last state ceremony of which official photographs were taken.

In the preceding Weimar Republic the various parties had recruited and educated young people along political lines, as future party members. In the late Twenties there were about forty thousand young communists in two separate organisations. The Young Socialists, one hundred thousand strong in 1914, numbered sixty thousand in 1930. At that time the youth section of the *Schwarz-Rot-Gold*

Hitler-Jugend

Opposite: Käthe Kollwitz' world-famous lithograph, designed for the German 'Day of Youth', Leipzig, 1924.

(Black, Red and Gold) – politically left of centre – comprised seven hundred thousand members between the ages of fourteen and twenty-five. On the right wing the *Jungstahlhelm* had about one hundred thousand members, and the *Kyffhäuser-jugend* sixty-five thousand. The *Bund deutscher Arbeiterjugend* (League of Young German Workers), the youth section of the National Socialist Party from which the *Hitler-Jugend* grew, comprised roughly

An enormous 'M' at the entrance to a 'Mussolini youth camp', 1938.

one hundred thousand boys and girls at the end of 1932.

It was a spectral sight when these groups of young people came marching through the streets, dressed in uniforms and carrying weapons nostalgically familiar to the men from the First World War whose interests they now served. Shouting old men's slogans, these youngsters attacked each other on the streets and in meeting-halls, and in such acts of

civil war young Communists as well as young Nazis lost their lives.

'Swift as greyhounds, tough as leather and hard as Krupp steel.' That was how Hitler wanted his young supporters to be: the right sort of biological and technical material for his coming war. The name *Hitler-Jugend* was coined by Julius Streicher, a former schoolteacher and founder of the periodical *Der Stürmer*, in which he preached his bestial form of anti-Semitism, with pornographic overtones.

'The Guarantors of the Future' greet Franco and the 'New Spain'.

Title-page drawing for the illegal youth magazine *Kameradschaft* (Comradeship).

On 30 October 1931 Hitler appointed Baldur von Schirach *Reichsjugendführer* in the National Socialist Party. Schirach set about creating an atmosphere of total communion between young people and their *Führer*, Adolf Hitler. While young Catholics were going to mass to celebrate communion with their saviour (who around 1933 himself began to assume in their minds the qualities of a divine *Führer*), the *Hitler-Jugend* was celebrating communion with their mortal *Führer* in gigantic parades. On 1 and 2 October 1932 National Youth Day (*Reichsjugendtag*) was marked in Potsdam by a parade of one hundred thousand young people, who took a full seven hours

to simply march past the jubilant Hitler.

'You stand behind me in your thousands, and you are I and I am you.' Baldur von Shirach, who fancied himself as a poet, put these words into Hitler's mouth. And another poet, Herybert Menzel, became even more rhapsodical in his poem 'The Leader Comes': 'Exult, ye millions! The Only One! The Hero! The Victor! Germany's new Eagle!' In the *Hitler-Jugend* religious faith and belief in the *Führer* both absorbed and transcended all old and existing beliefs in the church and the political parties. Never, since the children's crusades of the thirteenth century, had so much

Youth's trusting enthusiasm for the German 'Führer' (**below** and **below left**).

Political struggle gave birth to the *Hitler-Jugend*: hammer and sickle (**below**) as symbol of National Socialism before Hitler came to power in 1933; **opposite**: later youths marched to their death in defence of a Führer who had long ago betrayed them: final battle, Berlin, **opposite below**.

militant faith been mobilised in the hearts of so many young people.

To understand the overwhelming success of the *Hitler-Jugend* it is necessary to view it against the background of the Weimar Republic, with its establishment of old men who had themselves lost all touch with youth. Here was a movement that felt itself to be young, invited to fight to the death against a corrupt and decaying system that had outlived its time. For the first time girls and boys of all classes, from aristocrats to peasants, could feel their youthfulness being appealed to – their idealism, their energy, their untapped spirit of self-sacrifice. They represented the future. Tomorrow they would rule Germany; the day after, the world.

They heard the triumphant message: 'Youth is always right!' It was proclaimed to their elderly teachers by Baldur von Schirach: 'You are simply forgetting that, in a higher sense, youth is always right, because it carries new life within it. The only consequence of your obstinate clinging to the old life will be that you yourselves will have no part in the new. You will lose all contact with youth and with life.'

Quite a number of the youth leaders in the *Hitler-Jugend* saw the movement as a youth rebellion, a revolution of the young. It was a genuine revolutionary feeling which, though emanating from above, went far beyond what the *Führer* and the *Hitler-Jugend* leaders themselves intended. Several of the early youth leaders later joined the resistance movement, before that some had criticised the National Socialist party, accusing it of having become too rigid and corrupt. Their fight against the mandarins of the Nazi establishment was similar in many ways to the later revolt of Mao's young guards in China. These young guards had also been gathered, organised and inspired from above, and some of them developed a dynamism that went far beyond what Mao's team of leaders had envisaged.

Members of the *Hitler-Jugend* were deliberately taught to despise their 'old' and 'politically unreliable' teachers. In conversation Hitler would

HITLER-JUNGEN

often voice his disgust of his own boyhood teachers, who, he said, used to go around with dirty collars and unkempt beards. But he believed firmly in his young people. Many of the leading party members, he once said, had been taught by their own children to appreciate the aims of the National Socialist movement. Time after time young people had in their enthusiasm converted first their mothers and then, with their mother's help, their fathers.

The revolutionary fervour of the early *Hitler-Jugend* began to ebb in 1937. In December 1936 a new law had been passed. 'The future of the German people depends on its youth', it said. 'Consequently all young people must be educated in their future duties. The government has now decreed that all young people within the boundaries of the state shall be members of the *Hitler-Jugend*. Outside home and school, all young people will be educated – physically, mentally and morally – in the spirit of National Socialism to serve their country and community.'

Thus the *Hitler-Jugend* became a compulsory mass organisation, covering millions of German children. The consequence was that it swiftly declined into a sort of service institution, with obligatory duties to perform such as helping to bring in the harvest, clearing bomb damage, digging trenches in East Prussia and so on. In the final stages of the war Mills bombs were pressed into the slender hands of fourteen-year-olds to sling into approaching Soviet tanks.

In an attempt to halt the descent of the *Hitler-Jugend* into a faceless mass organisation, intelligent planners set about creating a number of special schools for the elite. In March 1942 the first 230 school-leavers received their diplomas personally from the hands of Baldur von Schirach, and the public could read in their newspapers for the first time about the new Adolf Hitler schools. Among the maxims of these schools were the following: 'Artistic, intellectual and physical education are equal in status'; 'Universal education calls for universal aptitudes'; 'In the Adolf Hitler schools there are no form books, no teacher's desk, no marking system, no impositions or detentions. All the paraphernalia of the traditional schools are done away with. That is their revolutionary significance.' Teachers and pupils used the intimate family form of address when speaking to each other. 'An important feature of the educational methods in the Adolf Hitler schools is that, in contrast to ordinary schools, argument and free speech is encouraged. Discussions are held on philosophical, political and moral themes, and in these the boys are delegated to put forward views from every conceivable standpoint. Each boy, whether he believes in the thesis he is representing or not, must be able to develop and defend it convincingly.' From a pedagogical point of view this certainly indicated a revolutionary breakthrough – but it did not happen until 1942, in the late years of the Third Reich, when hundreds of thousands of former members of the *Hitler-Jugend* were dying in battle.

Here on the battlefields, in the years 1942–5, the products of the *Hitler-Jugend* met the products of their Russian equivalent *Comsomol* as enemy soldiers. They had met once before, at the Paris World Exhibition in 1937, where the German pavilion had been crowned by a huge eagle (symbol of the *Hitler-Jugend's* great *Führer*) and the Russian pavilion by a couple of young workers with hammer and sickle.

In 1965 the communist youth organisations of Soviet Russia comprised more than fifty-three million children and young adults. *Comsomol* (League of Young Communists) itself had 19,400,000 members between the ages of fourteen and twenty-eight. There were twenty million children aged ten to fourteen in the Pioneers and 14,500,000 boys and girls in the age group seven to nine in the Octobrists. Only in China are more young people to be found in organised party groups. Rivals though they may be, Russian and Chinese government and party officials share common ground in their attitudes of pessimism and scepticism towards their young people. Both

Comsomol

are afraid that these youngsters will one day take a different path from that assigned to them. Both in Moscow and Peking the belief is firmly entrenched that nonconformists are morally inferior people, and care is taken that this article of faith is injected into young brains and hearts as early and as often as possible. It is evidence of the schizophrenia from which the Soviet Union suffers in its educational policy. On the one side is the need to raise young revolutionaries, the future bearers of the communist world revolution. On the other there is a strict and conservative educational system which kills all true spontaneity and initiative. It is geared to conformism, and its object is to ensure a smooth transition from youth to adulthood by means of political directives.

Comsomol was started in October 1918 as the revolutionary organisation of a youthful communist elite. By 1936 it had been completely reconstituted. An exclusive group of young revolutionary activists had turned into a mass organisation with a set of rigid training programmes. Its job was to preserve political orthodoxy and ideological 'purity', to pro-

Poster for the fortieth anniversary of the Soviet youth organization *Comsomol.*

vide technical and specialist education, and finally to guide and control the use of leisure under conditions of growing urbanisation.

Soviet children are told that they are growing up in the best of all possible worlds. They are taught to hate 'enemies of the people' and to love the Soviet fatherland. The basis of communist morality is 'Socialist humanitarianism' – the need to help others and care for the weak, the sick and the young. At the age of seven the Soviet child is called on to swear a solemn oath (the equivalent of baptism and confirmation in the old church) that it will love its Soviet *motherland* and the communist party. It swears friendship to children of all countries on earth. The young Pioneer loves nature (an echo here of the old German youth movement) and protects growing fields and beneficial animals and birds.

Educational psychologists in Soviet Russia regard the formation of character as a sort of tug-of-war between grown-ups and children. Their most important educational weapon is group pressure – the collective influence of children on the individual

Military discipline at a Soviet school.

of the same age group, which makes conformity appear to be voluntary.

A too bureaucratic approach in its educational methods has bred in Soviet Russia a spirit of resistance among its young people. The juvenile press is full of complaints about the dullness and boringness of speeches, which sound empty and are always the same. The schematic nature of orthodox Soviet political education may satisfy the party bosses, who fear the consequences of less dogmatic approaches, but it is of no use to young people who have begun to question things. In official quarters complaints are heard of 'nihilistic tendencies' among the younger generation. A small minority, it is said, has got into bad ways. In the past fifteen years criticism has been aimed particularly at the *nibonicho*, the *betsdelnichestvo* and the *stilyagi*. The *nibonicho* (a name formed by running together the Russian words for 'neither God nor the devil') ostentatiously disassociate themselves from any form of political direction. The *betsdelnichestvo* are the idlers who have no interest in training for the future. They want to use their free time in their own way, and they despise the career-building and status symbols of good Soviet citizens, that is to say, of their own fathers and mothers. The *stilyagi* are the Russian equivalent of British teddy-boys, exhibi-

The band of the Socialist Workers' Youth Movement in Berlin, 1932.

tionists who openly demonstrate in their clothes and hair styles their contempt for the orthodox youth programme. They hold heretically to Western standards of leisure activity. They love hot jazz, Western-style dancing, cocktail parties, English names and American slang.

The campaign against the *stilyagi* has noticeably eased since 1960. Official security measures against nonconformist youth groups tend nowadays to be directed along a broader front against 'un-Soviet attitudes' and against 'crown princes' who trade illegally in foreign goods in order to live like gentlemen. These and other young people – among them poets, journalists, actors and artists – are denounced as politically disloyal.

A comparison between the youth organisations of Soviet Russia and Hitler's Germany reveals certain similarities, but much more significant differences. Common to both is the direction from above, the drilling, the paramilitary training, the political and cultural conformism. But there is a contrast in the underlying philosophy. Members of the *Hitler-Jugend* were taught to despise all who thought or looked differently from themselves, whether they were Jews, communists or simply foreigners. The object was to breed an exclusively German class of young people to rule over all Europe. The word 'breeding' should not be understood in a purely metaphorical sense: to produce pedigree stock among its young people was a deliberate political aim of the National Socialists. The Soviet objective, on the other hand, is designed to appeal to children of all nations. It operates through the forces of reason, whereas the National Socialist system chose the emotional, irrational approach. In its basic humanism the Soviet system is superior to that of the National Socialists, since it believes in the power of reason, the human desire to create a better world. But it shares the same weakness of orthodox rigidity in its anxiety to integrate young people as smoothly as possible into the framework of the party and its political, economic and cultural programmes.

In both of these mass organisations the incidence can be seen of crises arising from loss of faith. In the Second World War young Hitlerites lost their belief in the invincible power, wisdom and foresight of their *Führer*. (In this connection it should not be overlooked that during the Nazi period and the war many young people from within the Catholic and Protestant youth movements also lost faith in *their* leaders – Christ and the Christian church.)

The Russian poet Yevtushenko has eloquently described in his autobiography the political and emotional trauma aroused in many young Russians of his generation through Kruschev's denunciation of their almighty father-figure, Stalin.

One single feature common to youth organisations and movements imposed from above, is that they all – consciously or unconsciously – try to minimise or even to ignore the real problem confronting them, which is the inescapable difference between the generations. Young Catholics were required to regard Pope Pius XII, their great father-figure, uncritically; young Christian Democrats in West Germany had to respect their leader Adenauer; young people in East Germany to trust Ulbricht in the same way that young Russians formerly trusted Stalin or young Italians Mussolini.

'The conflict of the generations has now been overcome. And that is as it should be, for youth movements have their uses only in so far as they are able to offer positive help to the state and thus to all generations. There is no place for them as forces of immature opposition . . .'

These words could as easily have been spoken by an American government speaker with regard to the young people of his country, as by authoritarian youth leaders in Spain and Portugal or church leaders in Germany and Ireland. In fact they were spoken by the *Reichsjugendführer* Baldur von Schirach in December 1936 at a press conference in Berlin about the new *Hitler-Jugend* law.

In 1964 an American, Allen Kassof, visited Soviet Russia to investigate the youth problem there. A Russian sociologist told him: 'There is no youth

Parade of the FDJ, the State-Youth organization of the DDR.

problem in Soviet Russia.' In other words there was no active and *recognised* conflict between the generations.

That is the great falsehood perpetrated by all conservative youth leaders who, both in the east and the west, attempt to use the young generation for their own purposes. They acknowledge the existence of young people only when these are prepared to offer themselves completely. The choice of a metaphor from the sexual sphere is not accidental.

It is here that the conflicts of the last ten years, between 1960 and 1970, can be seen most clearly.

Germany in 1945: after the war even youth had no other aim than simply to survive. Similar conditions prevailed in East European countries.

Youth problems since 1945

The battle of the generation gap, that state of active and passive civil war between old and young, has been waged unceasingly since the end of the Second World War, and its end is not yet in sight. But in the first ten years there was little outward sign of it. In a manner curiously reminiscent of the youth leaders of the Third Reich and the Soviet Russian sociologist mentioned in the previous chapter, experienced politicians and renowned scientists were finding – right up to 1960 – no cause for alarm.

The first post-war generation, born or growing to maturity during the war years, appeared harmless, if somewhat sceptical. It showed a willingness to adapt, was interested in completing its studies as soon as possible, finding a relatively well-paid job

The post-war genera-
tion in rebellion
against their fathers;
scene from a film of
the 1950s.

Soviet caricature of the 'American Way of Life', from *Crocodile*, 1959, **top**; caricature of the 'Uniformed Individualism', **bottom**.

and following in father's footsteps. Men from pre-war generations had found no difficulties at all in taking over the leadership of affairs – in the state, the church, the political parties, the trade unions and all social and cultural institutions. In the years 1957–64 the greater part of the world was still being ruled by men born in the later years of the nineteenth century. It is a significant fact that two of the most 'successful' personalities of the post-war period, Pope Pius XII and Konrad Adenauer (both born in 1876) belonged in outlook and mentality to the era preceding the First World War. Likewise the 'architects of a new Europe' – the French statesman Robert Schuman (born in 1886, served as a German soldier in the First World War), the Italian statesman Alcide de Gasperi (born in 1881 and formerly a member of parliament in imperial Vienna) and their Belgian and Dutch colleagues – were all products of the pre-industrial society before the First World War. Winston Churchill (born in 1874) was Under-Secretary of State for the Colonies in the years 1905–8 and First Lord of the Admiralty from 1911 to 1915; Franklin D. Roosevelt (born in 1882) was Navy Assistant Secretary from 1913 to 1920. Both of them were professional politicians and in many respects world statesmen, but nobody can claim that they had an eye for the approaching crisis: the effort of young people in a nuclear age to make their voice heard.

The *Encyclopaedia Britannica* of 1962 has no entry under 'Youth' or even 'Youth Problems' (the closest it gets is Young Men's Christian Association).

The truly overwhelming percentage of 'old men' in the leading positions of the western world was by no means confined to conservative, bourgeois or right wing institutions. Gerontocracy was equally a feature on the left, where ambitious young crown princes could only get on by a careful imitation and cultivation of the ageing 'strong men' at the top.

Stalin (born in 1879) placed the satellite states of the Soviet Union – Poland, Hungary, Czechoslovakia, East Germany – in the care of 'old fighters' like Ulbricht: men whom he had known personally since before 1914 or at least in the years of struggle between 1920 and 1939. In 1965 the central committee of the Chinese Communist Party was being referred to and criticised as an 'old men's home'.

Similar gerontocracies prevailed in the churches, the schools and universities, the civil service (which had an influence on cultural policy) and in the financial world (which made insufficient money available for building, equipping and staffing new

Sit-down strike of Munich students, 1968.

schools and technical colleges). It could be seen too in the trade unions and among those powerful European families which occupy key positions in industry, banking and trade.

The future was dealt with, on a purely political short-term basis, through measures such as the Marshall Plan (on the importance of which no reflection is intended) and institutions like NATO and the European Economic Community. In the west planning for the future was confined to the immediate policy of containing Soviet Russia and preventing the spread of communism by military and economic means. In the east planning meant waging economic and propagandistic warfare against world capitalism and particularly against the United States.

Both major world states, the USA and the USSR, frequently tend, in their conservative and reactionary way, to ignore the claims of their young people. Anxious though they are to absorb their young generations, they seem completely oblivious of youth's growing problems. And in this way they set the pattern for the dozens of small and medium-sized nations which are militarily and economically dependent on them.

Thus a huge vacuum has been created, arousing in young people the feeling that – politically, socially, culturally and intellectually – they stand alone and unrecognised. The four freedoms proclaimed by the founding powers in the charter of the United Nations make no specific mention of the human rights of young people (nor, incidentally, of the rights of women or of underdeveloped countries).

In the impending battle of the generation gap there are four main areas of conflict, each of which is modified to a greater or lesser degree by differing social and political characteristics within the continents, countries and social groups concerned. They are (1) the problems of young and old in an industrial society; (2) the problem of education; (3) the problem of sex; and (4) the problems of war and civil war. Within these spheres of conflict youth movements are being formed of a kind never before experienced in recorded history.

1. *The problems of young and old in an industrial society.*

As Peter Seidmann has said: 'Young people represent in their age group and in their own particular way just as much a part of the process of living as adult people in their various age groups and in their own particular ways.'

This sentence should be written at the head of a Magna Carta of world youth, for it contains a truth that the great majority of adults have not yet learnt to acknowledge. The state of being young is unique and unrepeatable. It comprises experiences, values and ways of living that can never be replaced in later development. A youth unlived is lost for ever. A young man is not simply a creature who will one day grow into a complete human being. That erroneous idea was held long enough throughout the European Middle Ages (which persisted in many countries up to the middle of the twentieth century). There was no special clothing for the young. The page, the farmer's boy, the solid citizen's son, the novice in a monastery (often enough a *puer oblatus*, a boy promised to the church by his parents in early childhood) – all these wore the uniforms of their respective masters, whether noblemen, artisans, solid citizens, or priests. Young girls were dressed like their older sisters and cousins, their mothers and grandmothers: they were deficient creatures, non-males, with only a single function in life – to marry and bear children and to serve a male-dominated community humbly and obediently in bed, in the kitchen and in church.

Many adults today react violently to the claims of young people to choose and run their own lives. Young people are both despised and feared, as are negroes, women, foreign workers and Jews. Modern adults are no more ready to grant their young people independent rights than the patricians of ancient Rome were willing to give civil recognition to the plebs – that is to say fellow creatures whose parents had no name or property and paid no taxes. It is not chance that has led many young white Americans to take part in the civil rights movement. The world revolution of youth is also a fight for the specific civil rights of the young generation.

The industrial society of today demands from everyone the ability to adapt to its technical requirements. Those who cannot pull their weight are eliminated – that is to say, they lose their jobs. Young people tend to object to this regimented way of living. Having seen their fathers enslaved and sucked dry in a lifetime of industrial service, they are not anxious to follow suit.

It is a situation in which both old and young are helpless. The old are frightened of being considered past their jobs at the age of thirty-five or forty, of being pushed out by the young. A German writer of the years before Hitler came to power, Hans Grimm, achieved gigantic success with a book entitled *Volk ohne Raum*, in which the Germans were presented as a people with no room in which to live. They had to fight for their room: in the colonies, or – better still – in the east, in Russia, the Ukraine. A similar psychosis now affects society. Many adults have the frightening feeling that there is no room for them. They are afraid of being over-whelmed by the advancing avalanche of young people, in the same way that the Germans were afraid after 1918 of being overtaken by the red avalanche of the Bolshevists or the yellow avalanche

Only a small fraction of the protest movement of youth has been canalized into social work. Sally Trench, who belongs to a London commune and who tried to help the methylated-spirit drinkers, wrote about her experiences in her book *Bury Me In My Boots*.

of the Chinese.

In the industrial society of today the struggle between the generations becomes a fight for existence in an ever narrowing space: in huge cities, concentrating ten to twenty million people in one industrial centre, or in huge business empires of which the individual can see neither the beginning nor the end. The adult urge to maintain his own individual place is to a certain extent instinctive. That the ancient cave man is still alive in us is a truth no modern biologist or psychiatrist would deny. But this instinctive urge is not lessened, but rather strengthened, by the conditions of the industrial society in which we live. Modern medicine and hygiene have raised the life expectation of each individual from thirty to sixty or even seventy years and more. The generation of forty to sixty is now a middle generation, which has to fight for its place not only against the young but also against the generation of sixty and over, which shows great agility and toughness in maintaining its own position. In the years in which Adenauer was German chancellor, politicians of forty or even fifty tended to look on themselves as young and immature, not to say infantile, in comparison with the grand old man who fought with every possible means to retain his power.

The anxieties of these middle-aged crown princes, still dominated by their elderly parents, are still further exacerbated by the knowledge that many of the young generation do in fact have the edge over them in the speed of their reactions and the quality of their minds. They have a cool eye for the main chance, and are quick to take advantage of it.

But the anxieties are not all on the side of the middle-aged and the old. The young too have their fears: of being considered not yet of age and consequently of being denied the right to take an active and responsible part in the social community.

2. *The problem of education.*
Nowhere in the world are schools and universities sufficient for the needs of the children born since

1945. In the underdeveloped countries such schools do not even exist, while in the industrial states – the United States, Great Britain, France, Federal Germany – the new buildings are inadequate and often out of date before they are even finished. They are too small to house the masses of young people who seek to make use of them. In overcrowded lecture rooms, in dilapidated medieval dens hopefully misnamed laboratories, on the steps of libraries in which every reading desk is occupied, sit angry and embittered students, a new group of *Volk ohne Raum*.

But even more important than this, the new schools and universities are not prepared inwardly for the young people who have been coming to them since 1950. In many countries the secondary schools are simply learning establishments in which masses of outdated material are shovelled like garbage into the minds of ten to eighteen-year-olds. They are not schools for life, as the best colleges really can be. Teachers and professors have themselves not been taught to understand the psychological constitution of the young human beings entrusted to their care. Outdated, insufficiently trained, badly paid and socially under-privileged, these teachers can make as little of their pupils as the pupils themselves can make of their teachers.

Such attempts as have been made by educational authorities since the Sixties to adapt syllabuses to the needs of an industrial society and to take advantage of modern discoveries in depth psychology, biology, anthropology and sociology, have either been too conservative and timid or have become bogged down in the planning stage.

Herded together, like soldiers in barracks, in closed buildings and campuses, the young people tend to develop anxiety neuroses leading to both inward and outward violence. Secondary schools have traditionally been the breeding-places of unrest since the beginning of the nineteenth century (universities too, indeed – since much earlier). Scholars and students have banded together throughout history in more or less illegal societies and groups to wage war on teachers, professors, tsars, emperors, kings and priests. And it is in the schools and universities of more than a hundred nations that today the new young generation is rebelling. In 1965 student unrest was recorded in over two thousand universities.

3. *The problem of sex.*

The school as it exists today (that is to say, lagging far behind the social demands of the present time) forces young people between the ages of sixteen and twenty-five into a position never before experienced outside closed institutions such as monasteries and boarding colleges in Britain and America. They are kept artificially in the position of children and deprived of those adult rights which were previously accorded to youths in most societies, whether they were aristocrats, workers or farmer's sons.

Discussion with Jean-Paul Sartre in a Paris existentialist cellar.

Even around 1800 young people of both sexes could reckon on being considered adults as soon as the outward signs of puberty made their appearance. Girls attained marriageable age at fifteen (in medieval times at twelve). Boys could join the Prussian army as officer cadets at the age of fifteen. Among the upper classes entry to university or to a profession was possible at the age of fifteen or sixteen. The school leaving age, and consequently the end of childhood, was raised during the nineteenth century to fourteen. Since that time the artificial state of childhood had become ever more prolonged. Apprenticeships, which previously began in the twelfth or thirteenth year, now start at the earliest in the sixteenth year, and entrance to the university between the ages of eighteen and twenty. Melanchthon (1497–1560) was a professor at the age of seventeen, Zwingli (1484–1531) a parish priest at twenty-two, while Felix Platter (1536–1614) began to study medicine at the age of fifteen and at twenty-one was a fully qualified doctor. An

Piccadilly Circus, London, demonstratively occupied by drop-outs.

academician today concludes his studies between the ages of twenty-two and twenty-six, while a medical student cannot hope to have a practice much before thirty.

The student today, whether he is sixteen, twenty or twenty-five, looks on his contemporary who has gone out to work and sees a free person enjoying, beside other freedoms, the primary human right of sexual freedom. Schools in Europe and America are all the products of former religious establishments. Fear of sex is common to both Catholics and Protestants, and the spirit of inhibition continued to linger on in the minds of the school authorities, long after the schools themselves had been secularised.

The repressive social tendencies which dominated Europe from 1815 to 1918 (and in some places up to 1945) had a significant effect on methods of bringing up the young. In particular, they led to attempts to inhibit or delay normal biological urges. Only people who do not know America can be surprised to find these old European repressions still very much alive in the New World – most noticeably among those in authority at the old-established colleges and universities. It needed the explosions of the years 1964–70 to break the deadlock.

In the fight for sexual freedom – put in concrete terms, the right of students of either sex to visit one another's rooms in the evenings – students have put up a united front. This is a fact that should not be forgotten in considering the revolts in Berkeley and Nanterre.

Over the past five years secondary schoolchildren between the ages of twelve and sixteen have been taking an increasingly active part in the struggle for sexual freedom. It is an issue of wide appeal to all young people seeking ammunition to fire against an adult society that persists in treating them as under age, yet claims the right to send them out to fight in wars and to use them as human material in the production processes of industry.

J

4. *The problems of war and civil war.*

The world revolution of youth is developing in a world in flux. The old forms of war are giving way to new, and in these there is a growing connection between attitudes to the enemy outside and the permanent civil war taking place within.

The Second World War ended without a peace treaty. As far as Germany was concerned, the Soviet Union and its eastern satellites came to an understanding with the eastern half, now called the German Democratic Republic. The western allies and the nations associated with them befriended the western half, now the German Federal Republic. Not until 1970 was any sort of treaty possible between the Federal Republic and the Soviet Union, or between it and Poland. The German Democratic Republic, like the People's Republic of China, is still not officially recognised by many western states.

The precarious world situation, starting as a trial of strength between the United States and the Soviet Union, became further complicated through the increasing influence of African and South American states, through the emergence of China as a nuclear power and then through the developing conflict between China and the Soviet Union. As a result, the many democratic governments set up after 1945 on American, British and French lines have been shown up as artificial constructions unable to deal effectively with old and new conflicts of a national, political, tribal, religious and personal nature within their borders. A hundred separate wars since 1945 testify to the state of permanent war which now prevails throughout the world. The victories of a hundred dictatorships or quasi-dictatorial regimes is clear proof of the real existence of a worldwide state of civil war, that can be kept down only by harsh repressive measures and glossed over by censorships. And it is not only in South and Central America, in Africa and in the Arab states that dictatorial regimes have established themselves. There is the colonels' government in Greece, the birthplace of European democracy. And there is

The thrill to shock: topless in Copenhagen.

France. Certainly in the France of de Gaulle censorship and control over radio and television were more subtly applied than elsewhere, and its preventive methods were less clumsy than the primitive concentration camp policy in Greece, with its prison torture. All the same, the French students and schoolchildren who swarmed the streets of Paris in 1968 saw in the policemen savagely beating them the same face of eternal tyranny.

Youth unrest in Britain and America

The first signs of unrest in the large cities of Britain and America came from young people of the lower working class and borderline groups which could find no place in the affluent society of the time. They were the children of immigrants, foreign workers and members of nations generally regarded as inferior.

A few years after the end of the Second World War boys from this underground society in Liverpool, Manchester and London, aided by others from a higher working class, set about the task of restoring their own damaged self-esteem. (Not a few of them had experienced failure in their family life, at school and in their first jobs.) These were the teddy boys, and they chose to impress their image on society through startling clothes and an individual showy manner of behaviour in public places. The importance of clothes as a status symbol is a phenomenon that has been encountered again and again in a thousand years of European history.

There was a cult of leather jackets, which have something sexy about them, though in fact many of these young working-class men from Liverpool and Manchester were puritans at heart. Still, they liked to boast of their successes with girls. Later, a cult developed for Victorian clothing. Speech, too, was important in establishing an identity. Teddy boys, beatniks, hippies, *provos, Gammler, voyous*, happeners, *capelloni* – all of them invented a vocabulary of their own, and usually it was a mixture of prison jargon, suburban dialects and idioms, and expressions borrowed from negroes and other 'inferior' races.

The musical *West Side Story* presented a romantic picture of the youthful gangs of Poles, Puerto Ricans, Italians, blacks and creoles which grew in the jungle of a large American city. Each gang had its own territory and was ready to fight any stranger who dared set foot in it. In the same way apes and other animals who live in colonies fight to protect their feeding grounds in the plains and jungles of Africa. In the same way, too, the fathers and grandfathers of the youngsters in *West Side Story* had fought in the era of prohibition, as gangsters, in the American underground world ruled by the mafia.

In America since the Thirties the job of bringing up children has been left to mothers, sisters and female relations. In this matter fathers have no say.

From the social underground emerged the Teddy Boys, the Capelloni and similar gangs in jeans and leather jackets, painted and hung with beads : an international rally in Zurich.

And the main worry is that the cherished son should not turn out to be a cissy. American women like their sons to have a certain amount of aggressiveness. The required quality, toughness, is preached in suitable form on the television screens through a constant succession of serials showing American pioneers fighting off Indians, gangster heroes shooting their way out of tight corners, and supermen performing spectacular acts of violence. It is a cult of revolvers and machine-guns, of the armed phallus.

After the mixed community of the pre-school playground, children at school form themselves into gangs, in which strength and loyalty are the main requisites. Some of their activities are outside the law, or even against it. But, as Geoffrey Gorer has pointed out, their escapades tend to be relatively harmless: a bit of orchard raiding, trespassing in deserted buildings, slipping into sports grounds and circuses without paying, smoking cigarettes made of coconut fibres, swearing, a little sexual experimenting, staying away from school and so on. The object is not to be caught by the police. In the lower and borderline sections of the big city population it is a short step from here to true criminality.

Structurally these groups vary considerably from city to city, often from district to district within a single city. But they all follow a single urge, which is to create an identifiable society of their own within the framework of an industrial society which has not yet mastered the problems of urbanisation and multi-racial integration.

However, such nonconformity remains the exception rather than the rule. As a survey conducted by a team from Purdue University among ten to eighteen thousand young Americans in the years 1941–56 reveals, the overwhelming majority of American teenagers were conformists. Born during the war years, anxious and uncertain, they came out in the survey in favour of a strong authoritarian government which would ensure law and order. Politics was considered 'a dirty business'. More than half of these teenagers were of the opinion that most

Hashish-Power
demonstration in
Hyde Park, London.

people are incapable of deciding what is best for
them. Sixty per cent were in favour of censorship.
They knew nothing of many of their constitutional
rights, or (if they knew them) disapproved. They
were quite willing to allow the state to defend its
interests through the police, tapping telephones,
banning newspapers and meetings, deporting un-
desirable citizens and foreigners, and so on. The
main characteristics of these young middle-class
Americans were seen to be fear of life and a profound pessimism.

In the late Forties American students were
showing less and less interest in political matters.
Among the professors at the universities there were
a few radicals, but the students' own organisations
were non-political, concerned almost exclusively
with internal university problems.

But it was in these very years, and in the Fifties,
that an explosive expansion began in the American
universities. The University of California developed
into a 'multiversity'. The silent generation was
followed by the beat generation, precursor and
progenitor of the hippies. The hippies were succeeded, and in part absorbed and transformed, by
the yippies, by successive waves of politically
conscious groups which often disappeared underground after a few years – to reappear later in a
new form.

The word 'underground' – a new idea for
Americans – was coined by the beats in 1954. Jack
Kerouac invented the name 'beatnik' by combining
'beat' with *sputnik* (the Russian earth satellite). The
beat philosophy, as it was to develop through the
Sixties, involved living life in your own way.
As George Harrison of the Beatles put it: 'No
one else can make you change.' Flight underground
was nothing new in Europe, where religious sects
had often during the Middle Ages sought refuge
from persecution in the catacombs. For the beats,
basements and damp cellars symbolised a voluntary
descent into the underground. They identified
themselves with Dionysos, Bakunin, Big Bill
Haywood, Trotsky, Fidel Castro, Rimbaud, Blake,

Baudelaire, Van Gogh, Chaplin, Rabelais, Wilhelm Reich and the Marx Brothers.

California became the American land of hope. San Francisco's Chinatown looks across the sea to Asia and the Far East. Here were the shores of paradise in a mild climate that allowed living and sleeping out of doors. There was plenty of unused, uncultivated land: abandoned land, too – deserted farm houses in which beats could settle.

The prophets of the new gospel of joy, love, anarchy and freedom from interference were Allen Ginsberg and Jack Kerouac. In 1954 Ginsberg 'discovered' Zen Buddhism. In 1955 he brought out his *Sunflower Sutra*. In 1956 Jack Kerouac brought out *The Dharma Bums*.

> This is the one and only
> firmament . . .
> I am living in Eternity
> The ways of this world
> are the ways of Heaven
> > (Allen Ginsberg)

This earth, begrimed and desecrated by murderers and machines, can be a heaven, the beats were saying. Our task is to find a way of living in heaven – here and now.

Allen Ginsberg is a mixture of Jewish prophets of the stamp of Amos and Hosea, wandering Buddhist monks, Zen believers and medieval vagrants. In American he fills the role of a guru, a spiritual leader for the young and not so young who are trying to anticipate the great American exodus from the damned and God-forsaken country of warmongers and war profiteers, of old men working themselves to death in senseless jobs.

At its beginnings in the Fifties the beatnik movement was not primarily a political one. But its pronounced and provocative contempt for politics, its refusal to take part in the rituals of party democracy, had a distinct political element concealed in it. Gradually beatniks and hippies and their political heirs, the yippies, came to the conclusion that older generations had turned America,

God's own country, into a hell on earth. Now therefore was the time to turn their backs on it and seek a new land of spiritual freedom, away from the cities, in the woods and along the shores. The spirit of Thoreau and Emerson came back to life in them.

The hippies

Drugs are supposed to engender a new sensibility.

Conservatives and reactionaries accused these young people of un-American tendencies or even activities. But what they overlooked was that here the old American dream was being reborn: the longing of a free man to build himself a life of his own on the virgin soil of the west, where he could breathe freely.

The first hippies made their appearance in New York and San Francisco in the middle of the Sixties. The word 'hippy' stems from the coloured jazz musicians of the Thirties, in whose jargon 'hip' meant experienced or wise. In the 'summer of love' of 1967 over half a million hippies swarmed throughout America. Children left their comfortable middle-class homes to found a counter-culture underground. For them the America of their fathers had become a police state, watched over by computers. Every human movement was controlled by the FBI and the CIA, working through a hundred thousand electronic eyes and ears.

The language invented by the hippies was an amalgam of negro, homosexual, criminal and drug-addict expressions. 'Turn on, tune in, drop out.' This was the slogan coined by Timothy Leary, ex-lecturer at Harvard University, for the new life of the Eternal Present. *Turn on*: use drugs and other stimulants to awaken the 'new sensibility' of the whole being, to enjoy experiences of one's own. *Tune in*: start a new life, choose another station on the TV set of the inner sensibility, seek other wavelengths of body and soul in order to hear the messages from the underground of the soul, of humanity, of the people, of America – and not least from the hidden underground of the Indians. *Drop out*: extricate oneself from the power complexes and working conditions of the ordinary citizen, from the slavery of supply and demand and maladministered authority. Young people who left school or university early, either voluntarily or compulsorily, were also known as drop-outs. In earlier years ex-students had often played an inflammatory role in tsarist Russia and the Balkans. Leary sought to establish a contact and a sense of identification between the hippies and these rejected social groups.

Like the happy band of poor *fraticelli* associated with St Francis of Assisi, the hippies saw poverty as a desirable state. All puritan creeds since the sixteenth century had regarded poverty as ugly and shameful: the poor, in the puritan view, were people rejected by God and rightly consigned to a hell on earth. The hippies, on the other hand, deliberately chose to identify themselves with the poor against the values of a godless, inhuman industrial society, senselessly producing worthless goods in a world full of poverty.

In their clothing the hippies adopted Indian customs, with their serapes, bells, beads, headbands and moccasins. They also took over Indian drugs, such as mescalin, peyote and hemp. It was all part of the expression of that concealed love affair between the Indians and the white people of America that has stretched from the days of James Fenimore Cooper to the Iroquois of Edmund Wilson.

In a peaceful children's crusade, bearing neither weapons nor cross, ten thousand hippies from America, Britain, Sweden and Germany left the armoured world of the white man in the late Sixties to journey via Turkey, Iran, Afghanistan and Pakistan to the India of the Hindus. In America itself the hippies set about creating enclaves, spiritual cells of the simple life in the heart of the great cities and in the freedom of the countryside.

All youth movements of the twentieth century have started with the feeling that older generations had failed to find any meaning in life. What does man live for? The hippies had an answer: man lives in order to love.

The word 'love', as they employed it, was a complex idea. Elements of the Sermon on the

Mount were combined with concepts of liberation, of cosmic communication, of tenderness towards all living things, flowers and animals as well as human beings. It was a belief in the silent power of transformation.

On the TV screens of America millions of people watched films of the operation called 'zapping the Cong' – picking off Vietnamese guerilla fighters from American helicopters. And so it was from a war sport that the hippies coined their slogan: 'Zap them with love.' Hippies saw the task of liberation as a game, not a battle. 'Make love, not war'. Love became the symbol of a new form of passive resistance, recalling Gandhi's *satyagraha*. It was the era of Flower Power: one must put flowers in the mouths of guns, hand flowers to policemen. The young people of Poland and Hungary had tried the same sort of thing in 1956, before Flower Power had come into existence: the attempt to counter the enemy with friendly words.

More important for the hippies than outward progress in space was the winning of inner space in the hearts of men. With the help of all available mechanical aids, they sought a short cut to those inner mysteries which mystics in east and west have for centuries been attempting to grasp in a lifetime of contemplation and ascetic living. A short trip with LSD or other drugs would bring them to the islands of the blessed. In relation to the materialistic culture it was trying to fight, the hippy philosophy was often nothing more than the reverse side of the coin. Consciously or unconsciously, their idea of the short trip to the inner world of joy, freedom and sensuality was based on the methods of the tourist industry, whose gaudy posters and prospectuses offer quick flights to paradise – fourteen days in Hawaii, the Bahamas. . .

It was the cult of the present (Nietzsche's *göttlicher Augenblick*, the *rien qu'aujourd'hui* of St Teresa of Lisieux). Nothing matters except today – and that means ignoring not only history, but the future as well. You do not wait for tomorrow; you do not rely on the future promises of politicians,

managers and planners; you 'do your own thing – NOW'.

The hippy resistance was directed against an intrinsically puritan and manichean form of schizophrenia which has marked the administrations of both President Johnson and President Nixon. This takes the form of dividing mankind into two groups: the 'children of light' (the good Americans of the white upper caste of English and Scandinavian origin) and the 'children of darkness' (the poor wretches in the lower class, together with all the red, yellow and black ones of other continents). It expresses itself in practical terms through the 'soft sell' for the white majority at home who are fed with luxury goods; and the 'hard sell' for others – in the shape of napalm, defoliation, poisoned earth and military zones of influence.

Unconsciously – almost, it sometimes seems, against their will – the hippies made three separate contributions to the political battle against the establishment. They created, firstly, their own style of living; secondly, a new way of conducting revolution; and, thirdly, a system of values opposed to the standard values of the ruling middle-class hierarchy.

In regard to their style of living, every word the hippies uttered, every gesture they made, every article of clothing they wore, as well as the manner in which they ate, drank, laughed, spoke, made love, walked through the streets, could be regarded as a demonstration against the taboos, inhibitions and moral codes of middle-class society. Every act was a

Demonstrations and disturbances at Grosvenor Square, 1968.

provocation against the polite manners of 'good Americans', who blindly pursued their work and their pleasures while the world around them was in flames.

The new way of conducting revolution was primarily a matter of surprise tactics. Respectable elder statesmen were shocked, confused and made to look ridiculous through some unexpected happening, often laced with swear words and obscenities. The purpose was to disarm pompous old men by exposing the hollowness of their professions of concern, their supposed objectivity and pious regard for the interests of pure science. Hippies turned the streets into a living theatre, creating surprise by spontaneous actions. Bare breasts against the warmongers: Jerry Rubin appeared before the Committee of Un-American Activities with the stars and stripes painted on his chest.

The hippies' system of values was an open challenge to the articles of faith by which the great majority of 'good' citizens lived. It created a complete set of counter-values: poor against rich; Indian against white; pastoral or urban-arcadian against urban-industrial; child against adult; youth against male and female; feminine against masculine; play against work; pleasure against pain; image against word; love against power; naive against knowing; communal against individual; spontaneous against orderly; anarchy against routine; self against society; empathy against reason.

The revolt of the Flower Children, with their gay, gaudy clothes for both sexes, failed initially, just as the crusades of German and French children had failed in the thirteenth century. At that time girls had been raped, and both boys and girls sold into Moslem slavery. Many had died. For the American hippies the year 1967 marked the beginning of the end. 'Peace-loving' citizens and policemen began to pursue them like mangy dogs. Hippy girls were raped by gangsters, thieves and bandits. In an entirely different direction, hippy clothing, slogans and habits were taken up and commercialised by the fashion houses of the establishment. In the autumn and winter of 1967 newspapers were proclaiming the inglorious end of the hippies. In the same way papal edicts from the twelfth century onwards had triumphantly proclaimed the 'final extinction' of various nonconformist sects in and outside the church: the Waldenses and Albigenses, the Brothers and Sisters of the Free Spirit, etc. These sects took refuge underground. The hippies too vanished underground, beaten, disappointed, dispirited and embittered, and most of them laid their flowers, trinkets, clothes and drugs aside. But a hard core went into hibernation, to emerge in the following year as yippies, a name taken from the initials of the Youth International Party.

The yippies – politically hardened hippies – saw themselves as free beings, dedicated to the liberation of the imprisoned soul of the American people. 'Revolution', they proclaimed, 'is always with us: we need only begin to live it.' They called themselves 'life actors' – with the task of altering conditions and creating issues.

American student movements

Student movements played a significant part in the political radicalisation of American youth. In the year 1968 at least 221 demonstrations took place in 101 colleges and universities (not including Columbia). In the period 1 January to 15 June, over 38,900 students were involved, 2.6 per cent of the American student population. (In Russia during the nineteenth century and early part of the twentieth century eighty per cent of the students were active politically.) In the year 1970, according to a report from the American Department of Justice, there were 1,800 instances of student unrest, including demonstrations, acts of incendiarism and occupations of university buildings. Eight people were killed and 462 injured.

Radicalisation affected only a small minority of students. In the march to the Capitol in 1961, the culminating point of the students' peace movement, eight thousand students took part. In the famous Mississippi summer project of 1964 in support of the civil rights movement there were 650 young people present. At the height of its activity the radical organisation Students for a Democratic Society (SDS), claimed to have twenty thousand members out of a total student population of over two million.

At the end of 1970 the vast majority of American students were devoting themselves to their studies. The numerically small groups of dissidents were split, dispirited and worn out, mere sparks in the trodden ashes. Mario Savio, the star of Berkeley, was earning his living as an assistant in a small-town bookshop.

Was this the end of the road? Anybody who remembers what 'tiny minorities' eventually achieved throughout the passage of history – in 500 and 400 BC, in the years AD 1, 1517, 1917 – will be reluctant to predict exactly what the social after-effects of the revolt of American students and other young people will be in the year 1980 or 2000.

In the few American colleges and universities established for the sons of the leading upper middle classes, political peace reigned practically undisturbed throughout the late eighteenth and the nineteenth centuries. But there was one incident worth remembering, concerned with the emergence of America's first political student leader, Theodore Welt, who studied at the Lane Theological Seminary in the Presbyterian Centre at Cincinnati in the years 1833–4. Welt, a thirty-year-old student of theology, was active in the American Anti-Slavery Society. At the college in Cincinnati he organised eighteen meetings on the slave problem. These led to a sort of revivalist movement based on a common feeling of guilt. Nearly half of the seventeen speakers were the sons of slave owners. The students demanded action: the slave owners should be induced by non-violent, Christian methods of persuasion to grant their negro slaves freedom. The board of trustees relegated all the students who were involved in the movement. These transferred themselves to Oberlin, and from there campaigned for freedom of speech and freedom of political activity in the universities.

Overleaf: Teenage festival on the Isle of Wight, 1969.

These young Americans from upper-middle-class families organised escape routes for negro slaves from the southern states to Canada. A century later their great-grandchildren were helping opponents of military service and conscientious objectors to escape to Canada and Sweden. American and British peace fighters deliberately went underground to organise a communications network, similar to the system existing in Europe in the late Middle Ages for saving the lives of persecuted heretics.

Every reputable college in America is proud of the 'rebels' who played their part in the nineteenth century in the permanent battle between students and professors. These were not political revolts, but internal struggles against college presidents and their administrations. Sometimes a complete yearly intake of students would be relegated. There were whole cycles of revolts at Harvard: for seven years after 1790, then again in 1807, 1823 and 1830. In 1808 Princeton expelled half its students. Princeton formed the centre for a deistic and atheistic opposition movement against the strict puritan and calvinistic administration of the New England colleges, which forced students to live puritanically and to attend divine service every day. In 1941 there were only twelve professed Christians among the students of Princeton.

In the era following the American Civil War the colleges were for the most part in the hands of benevolent theocratic and paternalistic administrations, with the president acting as a super-father *in loco parentis*. The 'children' in his care were, however, getting progressively older. In 1828 the students ranged in age from fourteen to eighteen. In 1866 the average age was eighteen years and two months, in 1875 eighteen and a half years.

It was not in the big state universities that student unrest made itself felt in the last two decades of the nineteenth century. The students there were striving youngsters from the less privileged classes, anxious to make their way by conforming to existing patterns. The accent of education was on the natural sciences and practical skills, and it was this combination of social background and faculty training that created, in 1970 as previously in 1880, a non-political atmosphere in universities of this sort. Student unrest was, however, rife in the New England colleges, where the sons of upper-middle-class parents laid claim to a greater degree of personal freedom, and where the main field of study was the liberal arts. In the years 1968–70 many students turned their backs on scientific and technical subjects – not only in America, but in France and Germany as well. They were more interested in subjects that dealt with human beings and their responsibilities towards each other.

The first political student movement in the United States owed its origin both to the Russian revolution of 1905 and to American capitalism. Its first meeting took place on 1 September 1905. Its founders were not students, but adults from outside the academic world, such as Upton Sinclair, Jack London, Clarence Darrow and the eighty-year-old fighter for negro rights, Thomas W. Higginson. But in spite of the efforts of some of the best speakers in America – among them Walter Lippmann, Jack London and John Spargo – the movement had by 1916 attracted only about a thousand students, out of a total population of a quarter of a million!

In the Thirties the student political movement started out as a revolt against the liberal idealism of the Wilson era and against liberal fathers who appeared to be too weak to resist fascists and National Socialists on the international scene. To these young American and British left-wing students the communists alone seemed to be fighting for human rights. The pledge made in 1933 by students at Oxford not to fight for king and country in any future war exercised a strong influence over the American student movement up to 1937.

Four hundred college students from the United States fought in the Spanish Civil War on the republican side. Soldiers of battalions named after George Washington and Abraham Lincoln, these young men sought to expiate their guilt towards the people and their own fathers through a martyr's death. After the defeat of the republicans British and American intellectuals, writers, poets and journalists who had fought on their side returned home disappointed and disillusioned.

In the years 1949–63 four generations followed one another in quick succession: first the 'silent generation' (1949–53), which was intermingled with a short-lived religious movement (1947–50); then a 'conservative generation'; followed by the beat generation; and then, finally, the New Left.

The New Left arose in Europe in the late Fifties as a result of disillusionment both with Stalin's form of communism and the reformist branch of social democracy. In Britain the *New Left Review* was established in 1959, the result of a fusion between two left-wing periodicals founded in 1956. The 'great awakening' of the American student movement began in 1960. The Young New Left declared battle on old liberals, old Marxists, bureaucratic trade unionists and the establishment of ruling castes with their philosophy of material success, pride and profit. The missionary role of these young intellectuals, and particularly of students, was proclaimed by the movement's spokesman, Charles Wright Mills: they were the instruments of social change.

Philipp G. Altbach has provided an apt definition of the student movement in 1970: 'an association of students inspired by aims set forth in a specific ideological doctrine – usually, although not exclusively, political in nature. The members of a students' movement, moreover, have the conviction that, as young intellectuals, they have a special historical mission to achieve the goals which the older generation failed to achieve, or to correct imperfections in their environment. A student movement is a combination of emotional response and intellectual conviction.'

It is a political mission with strong religious overtones. The messianic tendencies, which clearly characterised the young Marx, the French Saint-

Simonists and the early socialists in the nineteenth century, recur here again. Political activism means the revival of the old American missionary spirit, in which belief in a divinely inspired democracy is mixed with faith in charismatic leaders.

The fact that these young Americans chose anti-American idols such as Mao Tse-tung, Fidel Castro and Che Guevara as their father and elder brother figures should not be allowed to obscure their underlying emotional attitude towards their own 'corrupt' American fathers. The children of intellectuals, university professors, writers and teachers – the liberals and left-wingers of the Thirties and Forties – they grew up for the most part in open-minded, humanitarian upper-middle-class families. Their hidden motive was not the historically ever-present one of patricide, but the desire to see their fathers reborn with their old faith and strength renewed. In this deep and (more often than not) unconscious wish the mother had frequently a part to play. The importance of the mother complex in politics is often overlooked. It was active among schoolchildren and students in Russia, Bosnia and Germany in the period 1860–1940, and here it was seen again in young Americans, searching for 'the great mother' in India, in Africa, in the America of the Indians, among their own people: the return to the womb, refuge from the lonely crowds of the super-cities and the multiversities.

In effect it was a return to the great old American dream. The older generation had come to grief because it concerned itself almost exclusively with instrumental problems, with the production of material goods and values. This new generation, on the other hand, was deeply concerned with intrinsic problems, with the questions of identity and the meaning of life, here and now.

For these young people all the material problems had been solved – for the white upper and middle classes in the United States of America, but not for all the masses of people in both the Americas, in China, Asia and Africa, whom their puritanical fathers despisingly called 'devils' – poor, black, yellow and brown.

'The great American dream of "life, liberty and the pursuit of happiness" has been turned by a ruthless regime into a nightmare of death, destruction and the pursuit of dollars. On behalf of the tens of millions of our fellow citizens who have seen their dream betrayed, we convene today.

'In the midst of the corruption and terror of the past – and the present – we have come together to plant the flag of the future.

'Even as we meet, the rulers of our nation are sending off more planes, bombs, guns and gases in a desperate effort to paralyze the progress of history, to terrorize and destroy those around the world who hold freedom more dear even than life when life means slavery. At home, these same rulers enforce a society of fear with police dogs, cattle prods and prisons.

'The most hated government in the world today is the government of our country. In the remotest corner of the earth, the initials USA, which once stood for hope, have replaced the crooked cross of Nazi Germany as the symbol of tyranny and death.' (Paul Jacobs and Saul Landau, 'The New Radicals').

With this particular USA another USA is con-contrasted: 'the USA of the men and women who

American youths involved in the Civil Rights struggle.

sweat in factories to produce goods, of the house-
wives who struggle to keep the homes and raise the
children, of *the students, artists and honest intellectuals
who want desperately to create new beauty for life* and
not bombs and billboards for death.' (Note: My
italics – F.H.).

These sentences are taken from the constitution
of the Progressive Labor Party, formed by Maoists
who split away from the communist party in 1962.
The constitution, published in 1964, goes on to
state, 'We recognize that the fight will be long and
hard . . . We know full well that with this resolve
we fix our fates in a future of fire.'

The prophecy of 'a future of fire' was correct.
During the years 1964–70, in an atmosphere of
permanent unrest aggravated by the militant
reaction of police and federal forces, a number of
small cells dedicated to total revolution were
formed. It was a development confined to numerically small groups and to certain specific incidents,
but on a few issues these aggressive groups could
reckon on gaining, however temporarily, thousands
of ecstatic supporters. Such moments encouraged
them to intensify their deliberately provocative
confrontations with the police and other instruments of state power, and ostentatiously to defy
public opinion as represented by the 'silent
majority' of the American people.

The student movement was rejected both by the
workers and the conservative majority of the United
States (beside the Soviet Union the most conservative country in the world). It was also rejected by
the coloured youth and student movements. These
young white Americans, appealing to the people
and to their 'black brothers', received the same
hostile reception that the poet Georg Büchner and
his young revolutionaries had received in 1830
from the Hessian peasants, who denounced them
to the police. It had been no different after 1860
for the Russian populists.

The black students' youth movement arose
spontaneously on 1 February 1960 within the framework of the civil rights campaign. Four coloured

students entered a restaurant reserved for whites in Greensboro, North Carolina, and ordered coffee. When ordered to leave, they refused and were beaten up. The period of sit-ins began. Middle-class coloured people entered on a policy of non-violent resistance. The energetic leadership of a twenty-seven-year-old Baptist preacher, Martin Luther King jr., ensured that, before the month was out, this movement had spread to many negro colleges.

In part the rebellion of young black students was directed against their own fathers, whom they accused of having lost their self-respect after centuries of abject slavery. In the large negro universities, such as Southern University and Baton Rouge, some black parents even joined forces with the administrators to present a common front against the students.

In the following years the coloured students formed themselves into four recognisable groups. First, there were the revolutionaries: Black Panthers and other related organisations. For them the university was both a source of and battleground for revolutionary activity. Secondly, there were the radicals. They wanted the white universities to be reorganised, and separate departments created for black studies. They were prepared to see the white university destroyed entirely rather than permit a 'racist' university, which they considered an insult to their race. The third group were militants who demanded a total reform of the university structure, both black and white, and a redefinition of its aims and responsibilities. The broad mass of coloured students belonged, however, in the fourth group: the moderates. They wanted simply to get on with their studies, to gather knowledge and skills in order to improve their position in society.

The youth movement of black students attracted the attention of white students, particularly in the northern states. Civil rights appeared an object worth fighting for. A common front organisation was formed with the slogan 'Back to the people'. In the summer of 1964 650 young white people joined in the Mississippi project and volunteered to teach in negro freedom schools. The old American pioneer spirit seemed to be reborn, but this time the object was not penetration into the Indian west, but into the white heart of the south. These white students from the north wanted to feel what it meant to be black, they strove to merge in spirit with the poor, the needy and the coloured people of America.

Their overtures were very soon rejected, by the poor as well as by the coloured people. But before this happened, the 'revolt' in Berkeley took place.

In 1964 the University of Berkeley possessed the freest and most modern campus in the United States. The president, Clark Kerr, was a man of liberal and progressive outlook. One of the main causes of the political explosion in Berkeley was the social explosion that preceded it. In 1959 the University of California had about forty thousand students in two large campus areas, three small undergraduate colleges and a medical school. The state subsidy amounted to something over one hundred million dollars. Ten years later the number of students had grown to more than a hundred thousand, spread over nine campus areas, and the subsidy had been trebled. The university had attained the dimensions of a self-governing city, and the problems of 'governing' these masses of children who claimed the right to be treated as adults had become acute.

The mass influx to these colleges, covering eighty per cent of the young population of California, was a question of prestige. Young people who had not been to college were looked down on as inferior. Many boys and girls with no academic ambitions were forced by social pressure to attend university against their will, and their presence soured the atmosphere. They did not want to study, but to *live* and to find an outlet for all the youthful longings and fears inside them.

In August 1964 three students (two white and one coloured) who had taken part in the Mississippi project were brutally murdered. Though their white assailants were reported to be known, no legal action was taken against them. This event caused deep disturbance in Berkeley, and students adopted the role of the nation's conscience. Several thousand young people who were not students were living in the vicinity of Berkeley including a great number of drop-outs. In addition, a large number of beatniks had moved from San Francisco to Berkeley. The existence of this community played a significant part in the ensuing students' revolt. Not only did these independent young people have time to spare, but they already carried the seeds of unrest in their hearts. It only needed some outward incentive to set them in motion. On top of that, Berkeley had become a refuge for former Trotskyists and anarchists of the pre-war period and for relegated students from other universities.

At the psychological moment there arose a charismatic leader who drew all these restless and uncertain elements together like a magnet and gave them a cause to fight for. His name was Mario Savio.

Savio was the son of an Italian metalworker, and his grandfather had been a fascist in Italy. He had started his university career as a Catholic student of

Reaction against the left-wing revolution of youth comes mainly from the working class: building workers demonstrate in New York.

theology at Queen's College (Rudi Dutschke had once been a Protestant student of theology). At Queen's College the vital question for Savio had been whether St Thomas Aquinas was right. Now, at Berkeley, he turned his attention from Christian dogma to Karl Marx and the early nineteenth-century socialists. He became a teacher in the Mississippi project. Like many other fanatic young Christian radicals, he began to find the fiery spirit of the Old Testament prophets more congenial than the hypocrisies of the established church and its company of 'atom-bomb Christians'.

In the autumn and winter of 1964 Berkeley was the scene of a number of clashes between very small groups of radical students and the university administration. Policemen appeared on the college campus. At the beginning of October students surrounded and held for thirty-six hours a police car which had come to collect Jack Steinberg, a non-student member of the Free Speech Movement. On 20 November Joan Baez was singing about freedom and love: 'We shall overcome.' Thousands of young people marched singing to the university hall. On 2 December the students occupied Sproul Hall, the central administration building. Mario Savio got up to denounce Clark Kerr for running the university as a sort of conveyor belt of raw material to industry. In the occupied hall the Free University of California was proclaimed. New lecturers, new professors and new students would together work out a new programme of studies. In the night the police entered Sproul Hall and arrested 814 people, including 590 students. The presence of 635 policemen on the campus had an electrifying effect on the students; who saw them as a living proof that the USA had become a police state. On 3 December the students went on strike. On 7 December Clark Kerr addressed a meeting of eighteen thousand students and professors and promised very sweeping reforms.

On 8 December the faculty of professors went over to the side of the students, demanding complete freedom of speech and of assembly. Quite a number of these professors had themselves experienced frustrations of their own in the preceding years. They knew what it was to feel powerless against trustees, university administrators, McCarthy witch-hunters and the 'public opinion' of a broad mass of small-minded citizens casting envious glances on the unsavoury intellectuals, Jews and foreigners in their midst.

In the following years force was used in mounting measure. 'Obscene' political speeches introduced a sexual note of protest against the tabus of a society which was shocked by the exposure of a naked breast, yet unmoved by the violence and brutalities served up in fictional form by television and cinema and in real practice in Vietnam and South America. The student movement split into small groups of activists. But the common enemy was still the impersonal mammoth university, the machine which – as depicted by the student leaders Mario Savio, Suzanne Goldberg, Michael Lerner and Robert Atkins – was engaged in turning students into a list of numbers in the computing systems of heavy industry. 'Are you a student,' they asked, 'or an IBM card?'

Following the second great strike in December 1966 the Berkeley strike committee gave expression once more in its final communique to the students' longing for the realisation of the American dream. It was a call for a community of love, comradeship and brotherly feeling, its symbol the yellow submarine of the Beatles (which, taken over by hip pacifists in the harbour of New York, led to a peace parade of ten thousand people through the streets of the city).

'Last night we celebrated the growing fusion of head, heart and hands; of hippies and activists; and our joy and confidence in our ability to care for and take care of ourselves and what is ours.' The communique ended with the words: 'We love you.'

In June 1967 Mario Savio was sent to prison for four months. With him went many of his comrades – the scapegoats for two and a half years of strife. The most eminent representative in Berkeley of the conservative front against the students (in so far as such a front existed) was Professor Lewis S. Feuer, author of a richly documented book about student movements throughout the world. What seemed to have shocked him particularly, both morally and politically, was the fact that Mario Savio had not been prepared to admit until several months after the event that he had bitten a policeman in the thigh. Though I myself do not advocate the biting of policemen or anyone else, I feel there is something grotesque about the 'moral' condemnation of such an act, in view of all the brutal acts of terror perpetrated by policemen, soldiers and members of the secret service in the past ten years against men, women and children (including, again and again, students) – not only in Berkeley, but in Berlin, Zürich, Paris, Tokyo and Rio de Janeiro as well.

In April and May 1968 great excitement was caused by students 'taking over' Columbia University. The white students wanted to open their gates to the coloured people in nearby Harlem. The black students, however, who were pursuing more practical short-term aims in the full realisation of their power, requested the white enthusiasts to hand the buildings back. The white students did so, and there were heavy clashes with the police.

Two significant American reactions to the generation war as reflected in student unrest are worth noting. The first was the reaction of the white man in the street, manifested in a wave of anti-intellectualism sweeping from New York to San Francisco against 'un-American' youth. The most violent anger was evinced by the workers, whose trade unions always tend nowadays, in the industrial societies of both east and west, to support governments at their most conservative and reactionary. In America the intervention of the police against the students was supported, in varying degrees of warmth, by 86 per cent of the whole population.

The second significant reaction – measured in 1970 – was that of the men concerned in university life themselves: the administrators and professors, the sociologists and political scientists. As Stephen R. Graubard remarked, the students had brought the university to the testing-point, and there was no going back. Clark Kerr, president of the University of California in Berkeley from 1958 to 1967, admitted that the American university system still bore traces of its origins in the seminaries established by Protestant sects among the early English colonists. The trustees of the universities ruled over their professors in the same way that earlier members of the congregation had ruled over their priests. Though much had been changed, the university was structurally still living in 1900, and in some respects in 1636. Clark Kerr added: 'The great new force is the students.'

Morris B. Abram, president of Brandeis University, declared: 'We are currently in the midst of a revolution.' The issue was a new distribution of

War of the generations: troops on an American campus.

power within the social framework. The students were as well aware as anyone else that, while billions of dollars were being spent on super-armaments, the cancer research fund, for example, was becoming increasingly poor. 'The universities are in crisis because society is in crisis.' The restless, difficult, unpleasant and rebellious students of today were the great hope for the nation's future.

The Nobel Prizewinner Salvador Edward Luria and his wife Zelia, in a review of the American university system, declared that the university's only chance for the future was to take an active part in experiments aiming at a revision of society. The university must be prepared to risk its own arm in the social venture, which was one of colossal change.

Here was the word 'change', the magic word of youth and the underground, being invoked as a call to action by prominent university teachers. Luria and his wife added: 'In the United States student unrest is not so much a revolt against traditional values as a revulsion against a society that at times seems to betray its own proclaimed values.'

At the beginning of 1969 Professor John Somerville of California Western University wrote to every single member of Congress, putting the following question: 'Do you see it as a serious problem that the president undertook war operations on a large scale, as in Korea and Vietnam, without consulting Congress – acts strictly forbidden him by the constitution?' Only 9.3 per cent of those asked gave a reply, and of these 94 per cent declared: 'Yes, there is a serious constitutional problem.'

The same question is today being asked by a generation of young people anxious to know how the men in power stand in relation to the American constitution, to tradition and to war. As far back as 1787 Thomas Jefferson said that it was not only the citizen's right, but his duty to resist an unjust government that abused its own constitution. It was with an eye to warlike presidents that Jefferson and Lincoln reserved for Congress the right to declare war. Henry David Thoreau went to prison rather

A militant of the
Black Power
movement.

than pay taxes to support the war against Mexico and slavery inside the borders of the United States. At the very time Lincoln was castigating President Polk in Congress for making war on Mexico in defiance of the constitution, Thoreau was writing his famous essay *On the Duty of Civil Disobedience*. American students of today take the conscientious principles of their forefathers seriously. The American establishment of today – the politicians, scientists, businessmen, civil servants, judges, teachers – may indeed still pay lip service to Lincoln, Jefferson, Thoreau and others, but they seem unable to see that for their young generation a situation prevails like than in 1776 and 1840.

In 1970 Peter J. Caws, professor of philosophy at Hunter College and at the City University, New York, called for a basic reconstruction of the American university system. The American universities of today, he said, are all of them third-rate, and the whole educational system is fourth-rate – in spite of Exeter and Groton, Harvard and Yale. Administrators should be the servants and not the masters of the university, which should become a living and working community of people teaching and people learning. Students of eighteen are today adult persons, and they should set up their own programme of studies.

Caws called on the quality of creative imagination to refashion not only the university, but the whole of society as well. The rebellious French students of May 1968 were inspired by the surrealists: *L' imagination au pouvoir*. Imagination must take over power. That was the answer, but we should be under no illusions: imagination would have to work hard to fit itself for the great task ahead.

The response in Europe to Berkeley, Columbia and the American students' peace offensive was soon seen in Germany, France, Italy and Spain.

Youth rebellion in Europe, 1960-70

Western Europe owed its economic recovery after the Second World War to American aid (the Marshall Plan). That, together with the economic ties which arose out of it, gave the countries of western Europe their inner political stability. But western Europe also owed its post-war political demoralisation to America. The champions of democracy, political re-education and denazification came pouring in – their immediate aim being to help the professional politicians and diplomats erect a bulwark against the Russians. CIA agencies were established in Federal Germany, Italy, France, Austria, Holland, Switzerland, Spain and Portugal – and, as long as it was possible to maintain them, in Hungary, Poland and Czechoslovakia as well.

In the ruined cities of Europe, from Berlin to Naples, from Rotterdam to Rome, young people of the post-war generation began to form an underground of their own to place beside the existing underground of black marketeers, criminals and political criminals.

Some of these young people were organised in groups, but most of them were individuals. The vast majority of young people were more interested in studying, working and trying to forget the early post-war excesses of the occupying powers. But, above all, they wanted to *live*.

In all western European countries political and economic leadership was entrusted in the first years to elderly men with clear, or nearly clear, political records. However, as the cold war gained in intensity, men who had at one time in their career collaborated with Hitler began to find increasing acceptance.

Thanks initially to American financial aid, though eventually to their own extraordinary efforts of recovery, the countries of western Europe

Freud, Marx,
Marcuse: holy trinity
of the modern youth
movement.

had by 1960 re-established a high degree of political
and economic stability. But in the process they
seemed to have lost their European soul. They had
also lost their youth. Where were the young intellectuals like Peter Abelard, the young religious and
political rebels like Arnold of Brescia? It was twelfth-
century men such as these who had established the
revolutionary tradition that made Europe the
breeding-ground of the epoch-making revolutions
in the nineteenth and twentieth centuries.

The first post-war stirrings of youth did not
occur on the political front. That front was heavily
guarded by the serried ranks of elderly party-men,

professors, trade union leaders and church dignitaries, who kept a tight hold on the schools and universities as well. The complacency and arrogance of these men, and their ruthless ability in the years 1946–60 to make or break the younger men beneath them, did more than anything else to stir young people to rebellion in the years 1960–70. What outlet was there for them but to escape into a counter-culture of their own?

The Gammler movement

It began, unpolitically, with a withdrawal from the materialistic society of their fathers. The *Gammler, voyous, capelloni* and *provos* may not yet have formulated their ideas in words, but they shared the same basic feelings: that an industrial society bent, in circumstances of cut-throat competition, on producing more and more consumer and luxury goods, more and more weapons as

Revolt against the Soviet 'Big Brother State' **right:** Hungarian students during the uprising of 1956; **far right:** Polish students remember Rosa Luxemburg.

quickly as possible, was pushing mankind off its proper path. And young people were no longer prepared to cooperate.

At the beginning of the Sixties the first imitations of the American beatniks began to make their appearance in Europe. In Germany they were called *Gammler*, and they represented an attempt by young people to lead a life of their own outside the ruthless world of competitive capitalistic industry. They were the successors of the people Rimbaud had described in 1870 in his poem *La Bohême*. They wandered through Europe without weapons, possessions or money, sleeping in the open or in isolated barns, and in the winter they moved east – first to Greece, then the Lebanon, then India. Grouped round some ancient statue in the middle of a large city, they argued, shouted and

sang until the police came to move them on. Simply through their manner of living the *Gammler* cast doubt on the sacred values of a neo-capitalistic society. They were a living provocation, though they attacked nothing direct. That massive personification of neo-bourgeois society Federal Chancellor Erhard, knew instinctively, however, what it was all about when he said: 'As long as I am in office, I will do all I can to destroy this mischief.'

The west-European *Gammler* were mostly very young boys and girls from middle-class families. A statistical survey, which admittedly did not cover the whole of Europe, established that eleven per cent of the *Gammler* were under the age of sixteen, seventy-one per cent were between the ages of sixteen and twenty-one, and thirteen per cent between twenty-two and twenty-five. Only five per cent were older than twenty-five. Of these young people eleven per cent came from the upper classes, eighty-two per cent from the middle classes and seven per cent from the lower classes. Fifty-three

Hippy camp, Amsterdam. The site, the war memorial in the centre of the city, was chosen to challenge the established order.

per cent had attended secondary school and sixteen per cent had been university students. This shows that a high percentage of *Gammler* belonged in the category of drop-outs.

By 1967 the *Gammler* movement had already begun to decline. They vanished underground to emerge later, transformed, as small, politically orientated groups.

The transformation process can most interestingly be seen at work among the Dutch *provos*. These first made their appearance in the streets of Amsterdam in 1960: they consisted mainly of young men with long hair and beards, with their attendant girls. The name *provo* (derived from 'provocation') was not coined until 1964, at the same time as the word *Gammler*. Their emblem was the colour white. They were the 'white peril'. A 'white plan for women' was designed to shock aggressively puritanical Calvanists and bigoted Catholics.

Dutch *provos* pleaded on behalf of the 'white road' (against pollution of town and country by chemical waste and car fumes); the 'white man' (the recognition of opposing viewpoints); the 'white house' (open to all – and not to be confused with the White House in Washington!). The 'white bicycle' should protect beautiful and historical places from the ravages of the motor car. Amsterdam was to become the 'white city' – a place for men to live and play in freedom and to develop their creative faculties: the living quarters of *homo ludens*. In his book *Homo ludens* the great Dutch historian, Jan Huizinga, Queen Juliana's tutor, had put forward the theory that the ability to play was necessary to the fulfilment of a complete life.

Though in 1965 most of the *provos* were between the ages of sixteen and twenty-five, quite a number in Amsterdam were in the age group fifty to sixty. The *provos* appealed quite deliberately to members of the older generation who had remained young in heart.

In the local elections of 1966 the *provo* de Vries was elected with 13,000 votes to a seat on the city

The provos

council in Amsterdam. Speaking in Frankfurt, de Vries declared: 'We have no power, and we want no power, for power corrupts.' Another *provo* speaker, Leo Klatzer, said: 'We feel a sense of responsiblity for the empty husk which is called democracy. . . . We wish to give democracy a meaning and make it something worth living.' There was support for this *provo* movement in the press, and in November 1966 a *provo* council was held in Borgharen. In this connection it is worth recalling that Holland is the centre of another European youth movement which is today engaged in shaking the Roman Catholic church, that oldest of all existing institutions, to its foundations. The Dutch, as Emperor Charles v once vainly warned his son, Philip ii, owe much of their national strength to the independence of mind of their people.

The *provos* formed a cultural and political underground in Europe. The first centre of the new underground in Europe was London, a city which had already, from the sixteenth to the nineteenth century, been the centre of a political and religious underground composed of refugees from east and west Europe. This new centre was not confined to young people, though it drew its replacements from the ranks of youthful nonconformists. A 1965 estimate made sixty-seven per cent of underground members former hippies, and fourteen per cent pacifists and supporters of the Campaign for Nuclear Disarmament (CND). London was the main link in Europe to the American underground.

The underground can be defined as a counter-culture in a society that regards human beings as so much expendable material. It boycotts the consumer goods industry: 'Don't buy from them what you can get from your friends.' It has free stores, free clinics, job co-ops (employment agencies), funds, newspapers, farms, schools. There are free universities on the lines of the Free University of New York (1965). The underground press began to expand in 1969 and now covers almost the whole world: more than a hundred newspapers and

Right: Dutch *provo* leader de Vries and the anti-industrial symbol: a bicycle in the colour of purity.

periodicals have a total circulation of about two and a half million. Art is equated with living. There are underground theatres, films, music groups, living communities. Many of these communities and cultural and political resistance cells sprang up in the years 1960–70 in the very places which, from the twelfth to the nineteenth century, had been the gathering places of religious and political refugees: Milan, Lyon, Toulouse, Paris, to name only a few.

In 1968 Gabriel and Daniel Cohn-Bendit cited Berkeley and Berlin as the two shining examples that pointed the way to the students' revolt in Paris.

The German student revolt

The Free University of Berlin was founded with the help of American money in 1948 as a community of teachers and pupils. It was designed to provide the model for a new and independent university in Germany. But Berlin, which in the Twenties had been artistically and intellectually the freest city in Europe, had in 1945 become the least free. It was split into two parts, East Berlin and West Berlin, the latter separated from the countries of western Europe by the hostile territories of the communist German Democratic Republic. Within Berlin itself the two parts are separated by a wall, and even telephonic communication between the inhabitants on either side of it was cut off for eighteen years until its restoration in January 1971.

In such circumstances it was impossible for the Free University to become the bulwark of freedom it was meant to be, as distinct from the old Berlin University situated in the eastern sector of the city and now renamed the Humboldt University. Perhaps it might have succeeded in a small town in the Federal Republic, but in Berlin, the very storm centre of the cold war between the Soviet Union and the United States and a military occupied city into the bargain, it was evident at the beginning of the Sixties that it had failed in its object. To the anxious students it seemed at times that the fight for Berlin was threatening to unleash a third world war. As Adenauer's star faded, to be replaced by the obviously inferior regime of Erhard, the students found it harder and harder to believe that the battle for freedom was nothing else but a fight against the communism of Soviet Russia and the German Democratic Republic.

While Ulbricht was busy turning his part of Germany into a closed fortress to safeguard the Soviet Union's European winnings in the Second World War and doing his best to bring his own young people to his side, students and young ex-students in West Berlin and Federal Germany looked on with growing bitterness as the old men of the pre-war period consolidated their position in the west. Not only were they in complete control of politics, economics and industry, but they had also succeeded in taking over the new young army. As for the self-governing universities, these lay firm in the grip of a few hundred popes, ruling with the help of an army of subordinates whose 'prole-tarian existence' had been remarked on by Max Weber as early as 1924. As Weber pointed out, a semi-feudalistic, personal 'master and man' relation-ship bound these university slaves to their patrons, on whose goodwill they depended if they wished to pursue an academic career. A symposium set up in 1968 by the radical socialist students' association (SDS) to work out plans for a democratic university in the framework of a capitalistic society divided professors into four classes: first, the authoritarian fascist, who cannot be objective and refuses to allow argument; second, the strong-arm authori-tarian, who favours retribution and negotiates only to protect his own authority; third, the paternal liberal, who wants to be a good constitutional monarch; and fourth, the potential democrat.

These were the type of men who ruled over German university life in 1968 and resisted all efforts at reform with the ferocity of a cornered rabbit. The making of a German professor is a process of increasing social isolation. In later years only his fellow professors are entitled to address him by his plain name like a normal human being.

The students' resistance began with tactics of provocation. Their aim was to snatch the public mask of democracy from the faces of the university bosses and to challenge the political leaders' claim to represent freedom. On both fronts there were successes and failures. When on 9 November 1967 students openly scoffed at a traditional ceremony in Hamburg University, one of the professors shouted: 'You should be in a concentration camp!'

This was a familiar cry in Berlin during the years of student revolt, 1962–8 – and it came from workers, pensioners and ordinary citizens as well as from leader-writers in newspapers, who saw the fight for freedom as a simple struggle against communism. All who deviated from that very narrow view were denounced as traitors.

In 1962 students in Berlin began to demonstrate

After the temporary set-back suffered by the 'New Left' small factions of German youths join Communist organizations. **Below** and **opposite**: Demonstrations during the Brandt-Stoph meeting, Kassel, 1970.

their interpretation of the word freedom by collecting money for Algerian students. The occupying powers were not at all pleased to see the banner of freedom being raised against themselves. A Vietnam week staged by the radical SDS in Berlin in December 1966 ended with Rudi Dutschke's first appeal for 'extra-parliamentary opposition' to the existing social structure. At a demonstration against the Shah of Persia on 2 June 1967 the student Benno Ohnesorg was shot dead by a policeman. The publicity given to the funeral in Hanover, the students' strikes and demonstrations in Berlin protesting against the attempts of authorities and right-wing newspapers to gloss over the affair – all this helped to aggravate the feelings of unrest among

students in West German universities. The first signs of active revolt came from very small left-wing radical groups, with demonstrations in the streets and in front of public buildings. But special circumstances arose on occasions to win wider support for this hardcore from a broader mass of students. One such event was an attempt on Rudi Dutschke's life by a muddled youth named Bachmann (who subsequently committed suicide in prison). This act, which happened on 11 April 1968, led to disturbances throughout Germany in Easter week.

In May 1968 student demonstrations took place in many universities – in Berlin, Frankfurt, Munich, Geneva, Madrid, Milan, Rome, Brussels, Vienna

In the battle for democracy it is youth that shows the deepest involvement: West German pupils at a demonstration against Soviet Military intervention in Czechoslovakia, 1968.

and London, as well as at Stanford University in California. It is in this context that the students' revolt in Paris must be seen. But before going on to that, we might stop to recall some peculiarities of the German student movement during these troubled years.

Among the total population of Federal Germany forty-nine per cent belonged to the working classes. Of these six and a half per cent attended secondary schools and five per cent universities and schools of further education (as compared with thirty per cent in the United States and fifty per cent in the German Democratic Republic). The rebellious German students were the sons and daughters of the upper and lower middle classes, plus a few from the upper classes. They rejected their own natural fathers and chose their spiritual fathers from the ranks of prominent men who had been forced by their fathers and grandfathers to emigrate (in mind, if not always in body). Beside Marx and Engels there were the victims of the Nazi years, such as Adorno and Horkheimer. Others were Marcuse, Reich and Freud. The students also adopted foreign fathers such as Che Guevara, Mao Tse-tung, Ho Chi Minh.

But these young German left-wingers, who soon fell victim to internal dissensions and the hostility of the workers, were not indebted solely to left-wing nonconformists, anarchists and early Bolsheviks. To a significant degree they were also the product of that spirit of protest which had originated in the sixteenth century with Thomas Müntzer, leader of the left-wing Lutheran nonconformists. From the sixteenth century to the twentieth this much persecuted group had provided the leavening in the dough of pious orthodox Protestantism. A direct line joined the discontented pastors' sons of the sixteenth and seventeenth centuries, via Lessing, Schiller, Büchner and Brecht, to the young left-wing dissenters of the German Democratic Republic, grouped in Leipzig around the elderly Ernst Bloch and in Berlin around the 'young' Harich. Their counterparts in Federal Germany could be

Is there also a right-wing youth movement? First indications are given at demonstrations against Willy Brandt and Willi Stroph in Kassel, 1970.

zwei Willys zuviel

M

found in theological schools, both Protestant and
Catholic. The terms 'revolution' and 'youth movement' must be thought of, as far as Germany is
concerned, always in connection with theology and
philosophy.

Max Horkheimer, who began his career in
Weimar Germany, developed his ideas during the
Hitler years in America and then returned to
Germany. His description of lectures in German
universities was 'secularised sermons'. Now that
the Bible, the clergy and the high priest had been
stripped of their mythological associations, he
declared, it was high time to desanctify that worldly
church of the holy spirit: the university and its
dignitaries.

In 1968 German students denied their professors
the right to be regarded as fathers. In the same way,
centuries before, Luther had denied the pope the
title of holy father and had restored it to God alone.

The German youth movement of the late Sixties
also had something of the character of a children's
crusade, as the author of a book dealing with the
unrest that broke out in German schools at that
time recognised. The title was *Kinderkreuzzug –
oder: beginnt die Revolution in den Schulen?*
(Children's Crusade, or, Is Revolution Beginning
in the Schools?) The schoolchildren's movement
was led by boys and girls between the ages of
fourteen and sixteen. In 1956 children of this age
had fought in the streets of Hungary, and in May
1968 they joined very actively in the street fighting
in Paris – much to the surprise of their parents and
neighbours, and of the older students as well.

'A school is good when it teaches patricide', a
Parisian schoolboy declared in May 1968.
Thousands of secondary schoolchildren spread the
slogan: 'Power resides on the street, not in parliament.' By December 1967 half a dozen *lycées* had
already been brought to a standstill by an army of
striking teenagers. On 10 May 1968 the *Comités
d'action lycéens* (CALs) organised eight to nine
thousand teenagers in a demonstration that ended
at the barricades.

The great father figure for the marching students was not de Gaulle, but Mao Tse-tung (the 'wise Chinese super-father', as French Jesuits had described Confucius when they introduced him to the 'degenerate west' in the seventeenth and eighteenth centuries). De Gaulle, the new Louis xiv, had lost his halo. Posters described him as Hitler and his police forces as SS men. In the nineteenth and early twentieth centuries the intellectual fathers of the French students had for the most part been right-wing conservatives and fanatic anti-semites. De Gaulle himself had absorbed this anti-semitic outlook in the military academy of Saint-Cyr, which Pétain had also attended.

As a gesture of solidarity with Daniel Cohn-Bendit, the German Jew facing deportation, Paris students brought out posters proclaiming: 'We are all of us German Jews.' Never in the whole of French history had such an awful insult been flung at a world of French fathers who had spent their whole lives defending 'holy France' from Germans, Jews, freemasons and democrats.

The political poster is the great fighting weapon of French youth movements. In 1968 posters documented May as a month of renaissance, of world regeneration by French youth in France. In 1793 the artist and parliamentary deputy David had been commissioned to produce a series of engravings and caricatures showing how ugly, repulsive and ridiculous the enemies of freedom and the republic were. The French students and school-children who rose up in 1968 saw themselves as participants in a cultural revolution, a *révolution essentielle* in the interests of complete human beings. A poster identified it clearly with the Chinese cultural revolution, which had itself been inaugurated on 5 August 1966 with a poster proclaiming: 'Bomb the bourgeois headquarters.'

Of a population of fifty million Frenchmen twenty million were in May 1968 under the age of twenty-five. They had no voice in the running of their country. There were 514,000 students (compared with 123,000 in 1946 and 202,000 in 1961),

The French student revolt

Above: Title page of the West German Communist student organization's brochure *Spartacus*, popular in many West German universities. **Overleaf:** Rudi Dutschke (in front, with long, dark hair) gave dynamism and a characteristic profile to the Berlin student organization APO.

and they felt they were being treated like children. They were denied the primary human right of sexual freedom, which was enjoyed by every sixteen-year-old worker and apprentice outside the university walls. Nanterre, France's most modern university and an offshoot of the university of Paris, appeared to its students as a hell on earth, a clutter of buildings in a waste land cut off from all cultural communication. The students compared French universities with Russian factories, where the only purpose was to achieve norms laid down

by a central authority. Students and professors alike were powerless.

In the winter of 1967–8 Nanterre became the headquarters of student agitation in France. The university was denounced as 'a dirty education factory'. The students wanted to dwell in a living community, not in a barracks.

Among Nanterre's fifteen thousand students was a 'dynamic teddy-bear', Daniel Cohn-Bendit, the son of German Jews who had emigrated to France.

The romantics of 1844 had dreamed of forming a

The West German student protest reached its peak in Berlin.

spiritual and political alliance between France and Germany. Their aim was to free France from religious oppression (by narrow-minded chauvinistic Catholics) and Germany from political oppression. Young German rebels gathered in Paris – among them Karl Marx, Arnold Ruge and Heinrich Heine. In Paris, on 9 May 1968, a mass meeting of students in the *Salle de la Mutualité* overstepped the borderline between student agitation and political aggression. Representatives of left-wing student groups from Germany, Belgium, Holland, Italy and Spain pledged solidarity with their French comrades. Daniel Cohn-Bendit declared: 'There will be no lectures as long as a single student remains in prison.'

The revolution opened with a march of students and teenagers, waving red and black flags, proclaiming their slogan: *Libérez nos camarades*. It reached its climax at the barricades, where policemen forced the students back in a fight lasting four hours. Gas grenades were used. A girl who had not taken part in the demonstrations was set on by policemen in her own room, stripped naked and driven out on to the street.

Like modern St Joans the girls joined in the street fighting. The whole episode was a sort of spring awakening, a blossoming of youth daring at last to unfold. Someone compared it to the first act of love. Even its bitterest opponents acknowledged it to have been a revolution free of hatred, carried out in a spirit almost of merriment. Throughout the day and night people debated together, acting out their urges towards self-analysis and self-liberation. 'For a short time young people were united in a spirit of true Christian communism, and their veracity was contagious.'

The leaders of the student rising were between eighteen and twenty-seven years old. A few young university lecturers joined forces with them. Their defeat at the barricades was the signal for wider battle. What both the government and the communist trade unions had dismissed as an impossible nightmare now became reality: the workers pro-

claimed their solidarity with the students. A force of nearly eight hundred thousand people marched through the streets of Paris on 13 May and forced the trade union leaders to declare a strike. One of the students' leaders, the lecturer Alain Geismar, later declared: 'It was an unusual day. The students came out from their university ghetto to unite with the workers who had left the ghetto of their factories.'

At the head of the column marched Geismar, Sauvageout and Cohn-Bendit. From the middle of May to the middle of June France was paralyzed by a huge strike. 'It was the biggest rising in history, and it ended with a political fiasco.' On 14 May two thousand workers were on strike, on 19 May two million and on 23 May more than nine million.

For thirty-four days, until 16 June, students occupied the Sorbonne and operated a soviet of a very French type. France was to become a land of children and young people, a country of the future in which every young person would be free to develop his imaginative faculties. Posters pro-

Daniel Cohn-Bendit, the son of German Jews, becomes leader of the Paris student-left in May 1968.

claimed that kindergarten schools had been set up in the occupied buildings. A space in the Sorbonne was reserved for children to practise painting under the motto 'Learn to draw in a creative way!'

'*L'imagination prend le pouvoir!*' Young people would give freedom to mankind by liberating the creative imagination. On the wall of the school of art in Paris a banner proclaimed: 'The bourgeois revolution was concerned with law; the proletarian revolution with economics. Ours is the cultural revolution.'

From the elections of 23 and 30 June de Gaulle emerged as the triumphant victor. An overwhelming majority supported his plans for law and order. But it was a pyrrhic victory. He owed it in the first place to the French communist party, which condemned the students as Trotskyists; and in the second place to the broad mass of conservative middle-class opinion. The third reason for his victory was the historic impossibility of creating an alliance between students and workers within the framework of a highly industrialised society. Organised in their separate trade unions, the workers were out for a share of the existing order, which they knew very well would collapse without them. The students, on the other hand, were out for a complete change: they wanted to turn their spring awakening into a social reality.

The attempt failed, yet something remained. 'A spectre is walking the world – the spectre of the students. All the powers of the world have formed a holy alliance to hound it out of existence – the Pope and the Central Committee, Kiesinger and de Gaulle, French communists and German policemen.' Student rebellion was spreading like an epidemic – Berkeley, Berlin, Tokyo, Madrid, Warsaw, Paris. 'Students are gathering for a great battle against the powers of the world.'

In these sentences Gabriel and Daniel Cohn-Bendit were not simply parodying the communist manifesto of Marx and Engels, those two spiritual brothers of 1848. The two real brothers were proclaiming in 1968 the manifesto of a new class which would snatch the revolution of mankind from the old and icy hands of the communist priests who had strangled it. This new class was student youth.

'There are more than six hundred thousand of us. For some we are still children, but for others we have already become almost human beings.' These student-children wanted to join in the game of running society, and they were not interested in war games, in which their roles would be allotted from above. Their aim was free play.

The significance of play in the ideas of these young people must not be dismissed as frivolous. They treated it very seriously indeed. The *Union Nationale des Étudiants Francais* (UNEF) called on students of psychology at Nantes to give up their studies on the grounds that a course of psychology that did not acknowledge 'the innocence of desire, creative merriment, games and festivals' was useless. In May 1966 the students of Prague chose Allen Ginsberg to be their carnival king.

The Cohn-Bendit brothers demanded full equality of the sexes in their revolution of youth. The Christian-Jewish concepts of self-denial and self-sacrifice must be combatted, 'since the revolutionary fight can only be a game in which all must want to join in.'

Children were joining the new resistance movement. During the Second World War five pupils of the Lycée Buffon had been shot by the Germans for resistance activities. In 1962 schoolchildren had fought in the streets of Paris against the OAS, the radical right-wing French Algerians. The only fatal casualty on the students' side in 1968 in Paris was a schoolboy who was drowned in the river Seine while attempting on 10 June to escape from the police.

May 1968 saw student unrest in other countries as well, among them Italy and Spain. Though corrupted by fascism, the Italian middle classes still retained the dominant positions in society, economics and education which they had won for themselves under Mussolini's rule. After 1945 Italian students escaped into a life of their own,

Student unrest in Italy and Spain

fleeing from a rudderless society which seemed to them to be drifting apathetically in the direction of a third world war. It was a private life dominated by the three Ms: *mestiere*, a job – preferably well-paid; *machina*, a car or motorcycle – in order to escape from the soulless city, spreading its hideous new buildings across the countryside; and *moglie*, the wife or girl friend – sex as a means of escape from the wickedness of society.

Then, all of a sudden, the explosion occurred – much to the astonishment of the general public, and particularly Italian sociologists. In Rome, Turin, Milan, Pisa, Florence, Naples – the old traditional centres of unrest in the Middle Ages and later – university students streamed out into the streets, occupied university buildings and began to fight

A university occupation in Rome, 1969.

with the police. Their quarrel was with authoritarian administration and fascistic professors, of whom there were three thousand, holding powers of life and death over more than half a million students. The students' slogans were 'permanent revolution', self-expression, life 'here and now'. In Turin they demanded liberation from the tyranny of the 'book

god' – the rigid rules of syllabus and examinations. They wanted to establish a democratic system within the universities.

A survey conducted among the seventy thousand students of Rome produced the following figures: 61.2 per cent were dissatisfied with the prevailing atmosphere of the university: they had come expecting a freer atmosphere, only to find restrictions no less onerous than at home. A total of 90.3 per cent were in favour of protest, and 44.5 per cent advocated the use of force. No less than 85.6 per cent of the students were of the opinion that the educational system in Italy, including the universities, was in need of drastic reform, though 65 per cent felt such reforms were hardly feasible under the existing political conditions. Yet only 22.8 per cent of the students claimed to belong to the political left.

In 1969 the mass movement collapsed, leaving only small groups of activists, who turned to the workers for help and set about evolving their own system of schooling and self-education. Spontaneity, the magic word in years gone by, was now despised. Peace returned to the Italian universities, though sparks in the ashes could lead to a sudden

Jean-Paul Sartre speaks to student rebels in the amphitheatre of the Sorbonne, Paris, 20 May 1968.

new flare-up, as at Milan in December 1969.

In Spain, throughout the twentieth century the path of students has been anything but smooth. In 1926 they had fought in the vanguard of Spanish intellectuals against the dictator Primo de Rivera. Their demonstrations helped to establish the Spanish Republic. In the Spanish Civil War they fought and died, and many of the survivors finished up in prison. In the years 1962–5 Castilian, Catalan and Basque students staged protest demonstrations against a regime which placed its trust only in the sword, the police and the army. The student front was widened in 1969 and the following year by support from sympathetic workers and young priests.

A students' revolt in Portugal against the fascist gerontocracy of Salazar's regime was savagely repressed in March 1962. Participants were imprisoned, tortured, pressed into the army or banished into colonial service. In 1965, and again in 1968–9, there were anti-government demonstrations by students and intellectuals demanding freedom for the university and the press, the abolition of censorship and the right of free assembly. Banned books were smuggled in from Mexico and South America. The eyes of Spanish and Portuguese students were turning in the direction of their rebellious brothers in the American continent.

Right: Joan of Arc, May 1968.

Permanent revolution in Latin America

In Latin America groups of students and military officers wrestle for power on a volcanic terrain in which the ancient gods of long oppressed Indians and imported African negros are still very much alive, though they may make their appearance in distorted forms and under new names. An illiterate mass population is manipulated by a succession of overnight dictators, who often manage to keep on top for many years. But student movements played a large part in the downfall of the dictator Jorge Ubíco in Guatemala (1944), of Rojas Pinilla in Colombia (1957) and of Pérez Jimenez in Venezuela (1958), as in the civil war against Batista in Cuba and the removal of José Lemus in Salvador (1960). In the Dominican Republic students fought heroically against Rafael Trujillo, a man with the methods and manners of a Nero. In the years 1959–60 many students were tortured and murdered, but in the following year they continued their desperate battle against the military junta that succeeded Trujillo.

The university in Latin America owes its existence to the Spanish church. Lima, the oldest university in America, was founded in 1551, and Cordoba (a church foundation) in 1614. Spanish learning, at its height in the seventeenth and eighteenth centuries, held sway in Latin America right into the twentieth century, though in a rigid debased form. The arrogance of medieval university clerics lives on in the shape of professors who are quite often intellectual nonentities. Many of them regard their professorships, for which they may receive a small salary, as no more than an honorary post. Most of their time they spend doing other things.

But for the rebellious students the real enemy is the Roman Catholic church – an enemy which for a long time was regarded as unassailable. Though the church had given birth to the universities, it was equally interested in maintaining its position of authority in the state, and for this reason it formed alliances with the influential families and large landowners of the continent. It was even prepared in certain cases (as for example Trujillo) to give its blessing to dictators. Not until the accession of Pope John XXIII and the appointment of Archbishop Helder Camarra and Father Camilo Torres did young priests and Catholic intellectuals in some South American countries venture to speak out.

However, much of the intellectual arrogance of these Spanish churchmen had passed into their spiritual heirs, the student rebels of South America. They too adopted attitudes of intransigence, intolerance and terrorism towards the lay masses in their midst – the illiterate Indians, negroes and creoles. The anti-clericalism of South American students and intellectuals often looks surprisingly like orthodox political clericalism – merely dressed in new secular clothes. Each political sect fights exclusively for its own ideas and for domination of the university.

The famous Cordoba Manifesto of 1918 triumphantly proclaimed: 'Cordoba has achieved its own freedom.' This manifesto was to become the model

Father Camilo Torres, hero of the restless, socially committed priests of South America.

for all university reforms in South America in the ensuing years. But it was also the target for clerical and political counter-attacks in the years 1923, 1929–30, 1943 and 1946.

The new 'church of freedom' – the free university – had (as the proclamation of 1918 said) no need of outside rescuers. Its destiny lay in the hands of the students themselves. These students of the 1918–20 period were militant liberals, but there were also elements of messianism in their thinking, inspired by a revulsion against the First World War and a succession of civil wars in which philistine generals led unquestioning citizens and illiterate masses to slaughter. The students' aim was to turn the university into a citadel of intellectual freedom for all their literate fellow-countrymen.

The old university, according to the Cordoba Manifesto, had faithfully reflected the weaknesses of a corrupt and decadent society and its anachronistic regimes. It had been (and still was) an old people's home for the mentally afflicted (meaning the professors), in which all kinds of tyranny had been practised. It was a hierarchy of senile men, and now it was being assailed (according to the manifesto) by youth – 'disinterested, pure and unspoilt.'

The idea of the cleansing effect of a new purity is one that, at other points of time, appealed to the Scottish and English Puritans, to Saint-Just and to Robespierre.

The Cordoba students and their successors in the educational struggle in South America in the years 1920–70 demanded *co-gobierno*, a say in the administration of the university. The main aim at the start was to raise standards within the university. Incompetent and mediocre professors were to be deprived of their 'safe' chairs. But in later years *co-gobierno* became a weapon exercised not infrequently by all-powerful students' unions to secure degrees for their less talented members.

The more aggressive young people of postwar years sought their laurels in civil rather than intellectual warfare. Students became guerilla

fighters and guerilla leaders in Venezuela, Guatemala, Honduras, Nicaragua, Colombia, Ecuador,
Peru, Haiti and in the Dominican Republic. Che
Guevara's call to intellectuals, and above all to
students, to lead the struggle for liberation struck
a chord in many breasts. Che Guevara was himself
an academician.

Fidel Castro's rebellion started off as a student
movement. The revolutionary core consisted of
students and young intellectuals from the university
of Havana. Fidel Castro, himself a law student,
came of a family of poor Spanish immigrants who
had made a fortune in the sugar and timber trades.
One might say he transferred his father-hatred to
an adoptive foreign father, whom he could attack
without damage to his feelings. This was the United
States of America, which he represented as a wicked
stepfather to the Cuban people and all the other
peoples of Latin America. This wicked stepfather
was trying, through dictatorships and economic
enslavement, to weaken the people. Unwittingly the
USA played along with this personal imagery,
depicting itself on recruiting posters as Uncle Sam.

Many of the young South American rebels were
members of the continent's 'old families'. They rose
up against their own fathers as Russian boys and
girls had done in the years 1860–1917. This sometimes led to personal tragedy, as in the case of the
student José Manuel Saher, whose father, Pablo
Saher Perez, was governor of the state of Falcon
in Venezuela. The governor sent his son to a
religious establishment to be educated. The son
joined the guerilla forces, which the governor was
working hard to suppress. Bitter letters were
exchanged between father and son. The son became
the rebel leader Chema. He was captured by
government troops and, after spending two years
in prison, was sent by his father to London to continue his studies. José returned secretly to the
forests of his native country. In March 1967 he was
shot dead. Soldiers brought his body and laid it at
his father's feet.

Every youth movement, and in particular every

student movement, betrays concealed and complicated father and mother relationships. In both literature and research much more notice is taken of the political father complex than the no less significant mother complex. Very often the mother is invoked as an emblem of freedom, to become the open or secret protectress of her sons against the raging father. So in the Middle Ages Christians saw the Virgin Mary; and the Aztecs, humbled by the invading Spanish supermen, turn to their female gods. Both phenomena can be seen in terms of a longing for the womb of the divine mother of the people or – eventually – of the political party.

Similarly, one might analyse the murder of Trotsky in terms of a symbolic family drama. The young assassin adored his Spanish mother and hated his rich and conservative Catalan father. The mother left her husband and four children and went first to France, then to Stalin's Russia, where she was trained as a secret agent. Trotsky's wretched murderer was a mother's boy. She, whom he blindly obeyed, was for him the personification of the party-church of communism, and he strove to make himself worthy of it. Trotsky represented the feared and hated father, the satanic super-father who was attempting to seduce his young communist sons away from the pure truth, from the mother and, by extension, from the mother's party, the party-church of Stalin.

OLAS conference honours the memory of Simon Bolivar.

Young revolutionaries in China and Japan

The Chinese youth risings of the twentieth century – in the years 1904 to 1968 – took place against the background of a continuous tradition covering three thousand years, a period in which again and again the old men – the fathers and the mandarins – asserted their power over the young.

Amaury de Riencourt speaks of the 'inherent socialism' which had dominated the Chinese social system for several thousand years: a system which recognised the human rights of a collective body, but not (as in the west) of an individual person. According to Dennis Bloodworth, there was no Chinese word for the freedom of the individual until Sun Yat-sen invented it. Thus the paradoxical situation arises that the Chinese communists base their ideas on the very system they are ostensibly out to destroy.

Two hundred years before the birth of Christ, Shih Hwang-ti, the first emperor of all China, issued an edict: 'All official historical accounts are to be burnt.' Anyone found discussing forbidden teachings with others would be punished by death. 'Anybody who makes use of the past to bring modern times into contempt will be put to death

China

Mao Tse-tung, the great father-figure. Chinese poster, 1968.

along with all his relations. . . . . Whoever has not, within thirty days of the publication of this edict, burnt his books, will be branded and sent to forced labour.'

The book burnings, which occurred inter-mittently throughout the period of the Chinese Empire (221 BC – AD 1911), led direct to the great book burnings of 1951 and 1953 and to the icono-clasm of the Red Guards in 1966–7 – an unbroken line covering twenty-three centuries, from Mo Ti to Mao Tse-tung.

It was around the year 400 BC that Mo Ti gave his celebrated advice on the desirability of identify-ing oneself with a person of higher standing and the necessity of accepting direction from above – valuable maxims for Mao's young guards!

Communist Chinese interpretations of the ideas of Hegel and Marx are deeply influenced by the contrasting poles of Lao-tse and Confucius. This can be seen in the philosophy of Li Ta-chao ('the Chinese Hegel') and even earlier in Chu Hsi ('the Chinese St Thomas Aquinas').

It is to Confucius, 'the patron of enlightenment' and sponsor of collectivisation, that the Chinese people owes its deep inner repugnance for the ideas of democracy.

All revolutions in China up to 1966 seem to have been governed by the unspoken thought of the need to preserve. It was against this tendency that Mao Tse-tung's young guards were protesting when, in the period 1965–8, they announced that the People's Republic of China was being ruled by mandarins – by a group of old men in the central committee of the communist party. These old men, who had imposed a fixed and static form of govern-ment in order to allay their own fears of revolution and dynamic progress, had to be disarmed and deprived of their power. They were attacked and ridiculed, forced into self-criticism and self-condemnation by a group of young people acting in blind obedience towards the new emperor – the red-yellow emperor Mao, who had himself inherited the emperor's age-old fear of young people.

Right: China's cultural revolution. Large posters denounce the 'Mandarins' of the KP leadership.

In the years 1905–70 young people in China were fighting against their own fathers, who had absolute power over their families, their workers and their peasants, yet were too weak, too cowardly and corrupt to stand up to the 'white devils' from outside, the 'domineering' British and the 'arrogant' French. There was an element of love-hate towards their fathers in the resolve of these young people to seize the historical opportunity to turn their aggression against the wicked super-fathers in America, Britain, Japan and Russia.

It is not only in China, but in other parts of Asia and in Africa that the close connections between socialism, communism and nationalism can be discerned. Subconsciously these young revolutionaries transfer a very considerable proportion of their patricidal impulses to the 'white devils' from outside, the wicked stepfathers who throw nuclear bombs. It is the exact opposite of what is happening in North America and in western Europe, where angry young people deliberately choose their spiritual fathers, such as Mao Tse-tung, from among the yellow, black and brown people in order to emphasise their international outlook and to show up their own American and European fathers as inhuman.

Chinese students played a significant part in the downfall of the Manchu dynasty and the foundation of the Chinese republic in 1911. The second Chinese revolution opened in May 1919 with huge student demonstrations in Peking and other cities. In December 1931 a student demonstration in Nanking called for a united resistance to Japan by all available forces.

In 1905 China possessed one hundred thousand students in modern schools. In 1911 the number had risen to two million, in 1922 to over six million. Students had formed the first revolutionary cadres in 1903. For the hard core of his revolutionary forces Sun Yet-sen turned in 1905 to Chinese students studying in Tokyo and in Europe. At the beginning the young Chinese chose their spiritual fathers from among the white races in order to win intellectual supremacy over their own feudalistic fathers. John Stuart Mill, T. H. Huxley, Darwin, Kropotkin and Marx were the first prophets of the new Young China. From 1919 onwards Dewey, Russell, Ibsen, Bergson and Nietzsche replaced the old prophets, Confucius and Lao-tse, who were temporarily laid to rest in the subconscious to await rebirth in a new guise.

The first publication of the periodical *Youth* appeared on 15 September 1915. Its editor, Chen Tu-hsin, was five years later to found the Chinese communist party. Mao Tse-tung spent his formative years in the student movement. During his childhood he had lived in a state of permanent conflict with his father, a rice dealer who often beat Mao and his brothers and kept his workers on low rations. Mao was protected by his mother, who taught him to fight back in a Chinese way, that is to say, indirectly through a succession of hidden little acts of hostility. Mao lived and grew up deeply conscious of the power of family politics. To quote his own later words: 'The family civil war was the prototype for the political civil war of later years, even to the maternal lessons in guerilla tactics.'

Like their European brothers, these young Chinese were fighting against an authoritarian educational system and its teachers. Only a spark was needed to set the cause alight, and it came in 1919. The May the Fourth Movement ushered in the new epoch of China's history. In protest against the humiliations thought to have been inflicted on China at the Paris peace conference, three thousand students from thirteen colleges and universities in Peking gathered on the square before the Gate of Heavenly Peace. Heavenly peace had been the emperor's prerogative in imperial Peking. Now there was no emperor any more. Only after a long march would Mao Tse-tung rise up to become the new emperor.

The last virtual emperor of China, up to 1911, had been a woman – a wicked old woman, as the students saw her – who had been a concubine and had had to fight with wicked men and treacherous

mandarins to maintain her position. The students of 1919–20 were fighting for women's emancipation. In their theatre young male students were playing the role of Nora in Ibsen's *The Doll's House*!

The May the Fourth Movement spread rapidly. On 19 May the students staged a general strike, joined by students in Tientsin, Shanghai and Nanking. John Dewey was an eye-witness of this youth revolution. Like the Russian populists fifty years before, the students went among the people. They established workers' unions and set about educating the masses with apostolic fervour. In May 1920 a group of students from Peking university founded the communist party of China.

By now students were no longer being drawn only from the well-to-do upper classes. Among them were poor and needy youngsters of thirteen to fifteen, living in overcrowded barracks. All the rage and despair they needed to set them on the path to revolution and all the toughness they would need on

the long march to power, culminating in 1949, was building up inside them. Many of them despised their own intellectualism. Was it not intellectual conformity that, in the time of the mandarins, had turned men into the slaves and lackeys of the old men's ruling power?

The Chinese youth movement broke out into revolutionary activity in 1919, 1925, 1931, 1935 – always at moments when pressure from outside revealed the terrible political impotence of the young people's own fathers and the Chinese government. The British and the Japanese were the wicked foreign fathers who were pitilessly showing up the shameful weakness of their Chinese fathers. They sought protection, sustenance and truth in their mothers, in the womb of the people and the party.

The great cultural revolution began in June 1966. The seventy-year-old Mao Tse-tung was reborn, with the help of his wife. (Chiang Kai-Shek would be unthinkable too without his womenfolk. The

Mass demonstration in Hangchow against local capitalists during the cultural revolution in China.

women who played an important part both in the revolution and in the reaction against it are, as we know, members of a single family.) Mao resumed the role that he had held fifty years earlier: as student leader, in which capacity he led the battle of youth against the elderly dictators of the communist party. The cultural revolution began as a general strike of students and schoolchildren, though in a new form. The secondary schools and universities were closed for a year. The second battalion of the Red Guards was formed on 22 May 1966 in a school attached to the Tsinghua technical university in Peking. The headmaster of the school and eight of his 'reactionary' teachers were degraded to the position of school porters. It was the eternal schoolboy's dream come true – and also a revival of the Roman Saturnalia, in which social positions were reversed.

'Smash the old world to pieces and build a new

Chinese school-
children are taken to
a rally of the Red
Guards in Peking.

world from the ruins!' proclaimed the party journal on 14 January 1967. Young people came out in their millions to march, under the leadership of Mao Tse-tung, against old ideas, old habits, the old culture and old traditions. Their enthusiasm was immense: now at last they could act in their own right. The Russians were denounced as pedantic teachers, obsessed with examinations and hierarchical school systems. In one gigantic act of rebirth Mao sought to revive the spirit of the Long March of 1934–5, in which he, the new red Moses, had led his chosen people to the tabernacle from which the conquest of all China was to start.

'Emperor' Mao, author of a red bible containing all his messages of salvation, had now assumed the magic cosmic powers which were attributed to the emperors of Old China. Mao sowed the seed and ensured good harvests. Mao cured the woman dying of cancer. He was even present in the Catholic mass. Acolytes brought his red book to the priest at the altar. The priest raised his eyes to heaven, then read out Mao's message of salvation. Acolytes carried the book back to the vestry, and the Christian service could begin. (Similarly, in the Middle Ages, barbarian rulers were prayed for in the canon of the mass. And should we forget the non-Christian Constantine, who summoned and presided over the Nicene Council?)

Mao always helped – in life as in death. At a hospital in Shanghai a doctor told Louis Barcuta in 1966 that none of his new assistants, members of the Red Guard, was a trained doctor, 'but they are all excellently indoctrinated, and this is of advantage to the clinic and its reputation. You will not believe it, but these young people, who are not always able to rescue their patients, often make it easier for them to die by reading Mao's words to them.'

The 'children's crusade' of the Red Guards developed enormous powers of faith which made them ready to smash the power of the old men, not only in China, but after that in the two 'most reactionary' world states in existence – the Soviet Union and the United States.

Mao cast anxious eyes on his youthful supporters, who did not quite belong to him. He was possessed with the fear that had tormented the old emperors and tsars and also statesmen like Pobedonostsev, who had exercised virtually complete control over the Tsars Alexander III and Nicholas II in the years 1881–1904. In his famous conversations with Edgar Snow, Mao Tse-tung recalled that he had been a democrat in his early years, not a communist. He could not say in which direction the young generation would turn. They might decide to continue the revolutionary progress towards communism. They might, on the other hand, opt for a counter-revolution, make peace with the imperialists and bring the Chiang Kai-shek people back from Formosa to the mainland. Future events, Mao said, would be decided by future generations, acting under the influence of circumstances no one could now foresee. Living conditions were changing throughout the world with increasing rapidity. In a thousand years' time, Mao reflected, even Marx, Engels and Lenin might perhaps look rather ridiculous.

It was an extraordinary confession to make. But the grand old man of China, one of the most influential beings in the world – a man who had created a youth movement out of nothing and led the campaign of millions of young people for many years – was saying no more than what every member of the older generation must acknowledge, whether they are teachers, professors, politicians, political scientists, psychiatrists or just plain fathers: namely, that they do not know what young people will be doing tomorrow.

Mao Tse-tung was in fact experiencing the same feeling as any other elderly teacher or politician searching his soul after prolonged contact with people of a younger generation: they become aware of being alone. The word 'alone' crops up in Edgar Snow's reports, and in Malraux's account of his meeting with Mao it occurs twice towards the end. 'I am alone with the masses and I am waiting.' And, a little later: 'I am alone.'

Japan

The islands of Japan are frequently visited by earthquakes, and earthquake is the unconscious background to the Japanese soul, in which the fears, cruelties, urges and longings of an age-old past are thinly concealed beneath a veneer of western civilisation. At the present time the Japanese explosion is predominantly economic: in the past few years Japan has raised itself to the position of one of the leading industrial powers in the world. But in the wage scale it occupies, by world standards, the twenty-seventh place. Japan is still ruled by a feudal caste system. Members of the grand old families have managed – very successfully from their own point of view – to create mammoth industrial concerns in which hundreds of thousands of workers are little more than serfs. That may be a disadvantage to the workers, but (as tied peasants discovered in medieval times) it can have certain advantages in times of crisis. They are not dismissed but retained by the firm – at lower wages, of course.

The Japanese workers present no revolutionary danger, but their potential as a national force is great. In Japan's renewed struggle for domination in Asia – carried on now with economic weapons after the military attempt failed in 1945 – the workers' potential is an enormously significant factor. Faced with this tense situation, what will the young people of Japan do? Will they restore the old emperor to life in a suicidal attempt to revive the messianic spirit of Japanese imperialism? Or will they continue with the process of self-laceration in which at the moment some of their most active forces are engaged?

Year by year the numbers of Japan's academic proletariat are growing. Thousands of poor families are making severe sacrifices in order to send at least one of their sons to the university. Of the 120,000 students graduating yearly, only half can find employment to match their qualifications and expectations. In 1940 there were forty-seven universities in Japan. In 1960 there were two hundred and thirty-six universities offering four-year courses and two hundred and seventy-four other colleges. This development was due in part to the American occupation and its educational policy. But it was also in part a spontaneous Japanese reaction to the challenge posed by the very fact of American occupation. Never before in all its history had Japan's holy soil been trodden by foreign conquerors. The imposition of an American form of democracy represented for the Japanese a desecration of their fathers. It is a national disgrace of which the implications cannot yet be seen. Nations can nurse their psychic wounds for centuries. Even the North Americans, those 'people without a history' have not yet come fully to terms with their Indian past and their civil war of a century ago.

The reaction of Japanese students to the traumatic experience of defeat was at the beginning surprisingly practical and far-seeing. At a meeting in Tokyo on 5 December 1945 poor, undernourished and tuberculous students did not demand material improvements so much as political ones: the removal of fascistic and incompetent professors, and participation in the reform of the educational system. A five day general strike in June 1948, involving two hundred thousand students and 133 government schools, was directed primarily against the raising of school fees.

In September 1948 more than three hundred thousand students from 145 separate universities organised themselves into the All-Japan Federation of Student Self-Government Associations. These became known as the *Zengakuren*, an abbreviation of their full Japanese title *Zen Nihon Gakusei Jichikai Sorengo*. The young boys and girls who assumed the leadership of this vast student movement were fighting actively against their own fathers as well as against teachers and professors who had turned overnight from ardent nationalists to convinced democrats; and against politicians like the prime minister Kishi (arrested on a charge of committing major war crimes and then, after three years in prison, released without a trial), who had come to terms with their American military overlords. The *Zengakuren* were also at loggerheads with the trade union leaders, who had more than once rejected their offers of financial aid for striking workers; and against the elderly leaders of the Japanese communist party who had not been impressed by Krushchev's denunciation of Stalin. The *Zengakuren* themselves had been deeply affected by the disclosures. Many of their founder members had been close to the communist party.

In the years 1956–8 the *Zengakuren* officially severed their bonds with the Japanese communist party. Loyal party members denounced them as Trotskyists and American agents, while American politicians accused them of being the servants of Moscow. The *Zengakuren* themselves were, in fact, deeply distrustful of all father figures, whether in Moscow, Washington, Tokyo or Peking (they criticised Mao Tse-tung as being too conservative). And they reinforced their protests against the Americans with the rallying cry: 'No more worshipping the emperor.'

Their militant pacifism owed something to their realisation that the Islands of Japan could not be defended against American and Chinese nuclear bombs. They suffered from a sense of spiritual isolation. Many of them were highly educated young people. They read Marx and Engels in the original German, were familiar with Wordsworth and the other great early romantic English poets, as well as with Heine, Pushkin, Chekhov and Turgenev. *Utagoe Undo*, the group song movement established in 1950, found rapid acceptance among them. At demonstrations and at the funerals of members who had died fighting for their cause they sang new songs with titles like 'The Song of Happiness' and 'Let us Link the World together with a Wreath of Flowers'. It was a folk song movement in the spirit of the American hippies and yippies.

Professor Toshio Kamba's daughter Michiko was a member of the *Zengakuren*. In 1959 the old professor reproached his daughter: 'You are following in the footsteps of the Russian populists, whose idealism and heroism ended in Bolshevism. With your terroristic acts you are preparing the way for a terrorist regime that will destroy you first of all.' A year later Michiko was killed in the severe fighting that raged for months between the police and the *Zengakuren*. Toshio Kamba wrote a moving book in memory of his daughter. In 1967 Michiko's mother wrote an open letter to a leader of the movement: 'You have no right to call on the name of my daughter. She was pure in heart, whereas you have turned into criminals and gangsters.'

By 1963 the *Zengakuren* had split up into nine separate factions, all at odds with one another. With economic boom a new generation of young people arose, and these – on the surface at any rate – were not interested in the spiritual difficulties of their older brothers and sisters, with their obsession for diplomas and their examination neuroses. The new generation was able to look the enemy – the white and red foreigner – steadily and coolly in the eye.

In the present explosive state of humanity, in which men neither know their own minds, nor dare to examine them, the attitude of Japanese youth is one of the most disturbing features. Which way will they direct their dangerous strength when another crisis emerges, within Japan or in the larger world outside? Some experienced experts in Japanese affairs think it very possible that there might be a resurgence of faith in the emperor – not in the form of a new Mikado from the existing royal family, but as an abstract principle, a missionary vision of a Japanese-dominated Asia.

But there is another possibility. Out of the ruins of the Japanese student movement small groups of young men and women are emerging who believe in the idea of world revolution. They see an important task ahead for the young Japanese intellectuals who are having now to train themselves as professional revolutionaries in secret societies and other organisations. Their aim is to join hands with their brothers – first of all in China and other countries in Asia, after that in Africa and South America – to change the face of the earth. Inspired by all the revolutionaries and visionaries of Europe who preceded them, they wish to create a peaceful world community of free people: not only on the surface, as in the World Exhibition in Tokyo in 1968–9, but within the thoughts and feelings of men everywhere.

There is a 'Japanese dream' just as potent as the 'American dream' of today and yesterday. It has many faces and lives deep down in the subconscious of a restless young generation which is an enigma to itself as well as to its many older enemies. Nobody can say whether these young people will eventually be provoked by the rigours of daily life and the alarms and excursions of political developments to assert themselves, or whether they will fall victim to another future leader like that well-known Japanese writer and Nobel Prize candidate who took his own life in November 1970 because he did not succeed, with the help of fanatic young friends, in gaining power. As one of his supporters told me, he had wanted to 'cleanse Japan's tarnished face and to bring the emperor back to life.'

Enormous posters of the Zengakure organization with anti-American slogans at Waseda university, Tokyo. **Overleaf:** A civil war situation has also developed in Japan: Zengakure cadres against a police water-cannon.

A look at the present and future

In a period of human history in which people, as never before, have the opportunity to enjoy life in the material sense to the full, many students are being educated up to a standard for which there is insufficient outlet in terms of work. An 'academic proletariat' is being created, even in the old-established European countries with traditional systems of training and job-finding. One has only to observe the despair on the faces of young European students armed with degrees in philosophy as they chase in vain the few worthwhile opportunities in publishing, the press, radio, television and cultural institutions, to realise what is happening.

The despair of these European students is matched by African academicians who, having studied in Europe, have lost touch with their domestic customs and with their fathers, both black and white. In their own country a rival clan or tribe has possibly come into power. And even if, in their absence abroad, there has been no change of government at home, they are likely to find all available positions filled on their return. What is lacking in these countries is a broad middle class which could absorb their rootless intellectuals. African students not infrequently develop an attitude of hatred, directed not only against their own black fathers, who had learned to live with the colonial bosses, but against their white spiritual fathers as well. Nearly all the black African leaders of today are former mission boys, brought up in French and Belgian Catholic schools or English Protestant schools. They admired the civilisation of the white man, but at the same time hated it for its position of superiority. Conscious of their estrangement from their own tribal culture, many fled back to it for protection, became leaders of nationalistic secret societies and, once raised to power, became ardent supporters of a 'national' policy based on the old tribal system. Kwame Nkrumah, Jomo Kenyatta and Julius Nyerere are only three out of about a dozen African government leaders who began their careers as youth or student leaders.

African students are often conscious of their resemblance to the young Russian populists of the nineteenth century. They too experienced an unrequited love affair with their own people. Their countrymen, still in the power of old spiritual traditions, want to use the white man's technical skills to retain their archaic magic. Instead of western-type democracy, secret societies emerge, perpetuating in modern guises mystical conceptions of blood-brotherhood. The state leader surrounds himself with members of his own tribe and blood-brothers in order to maintain ascendancy over other tribes in his territory, and over 'rebellious' young students and intellectuals for whom he can find no use.

There are discontented young generations too in Korea and Persia, in the Near, Middle and Far East. Only in India are student organisations devoting their energies mainly to internal university problems. In the Arab countries – or at any rate in those smaller ones living in the shadow of Egypt – it has been found possible to channel youthful discontent into the struggle against Israel and 'American capital'. This deliberate policy of teaching their own young people, from babies to students, to hate the 'Zionist Jews' has helped considerably to relieve the weak Arab leaders and politicians in their efforts to maintain internal order.

As for Israel itself, we have already seen to what extent its early development was influenced by the ideas of the German youth movement, brought to Palestine by Theodor Herzl and thousands of young Jewish emigrants from Germany, Bohemia and Austria. Now these elderly founder-members sit rather isolated in their *kibbutzim*, reading their old German books. Their children cannot really understand them. Why did they not fight against Hitler, indeed against the persecutions in eastern

Europe, long before Eichmann and Hitler? But, though this conflict of the generations may lead at times to personal and domestic tragedy, it is of little significance to the state of Israel. The task of trying to protect two and a half million people against eighty million Arabs holds old and young firmly together.

The position of young Jews in Europe and America has developed very differently. In the Thirties and before, their struggles against their orthodox fathers and their abandonment of the parental home in Poland, Russia, the Ukraine, Latvia and Lithuania, had turned many young Jews into socialist and communist revolutionaries. Communism and socialism in Europe, the American student movements of the Sixties as well as their intellectual forerunners in the Thirties owe much to the leavening of Jewish thought. Jewish socialists and communists such as Heine, Marx and Trotsky set their seal on the political parties of Russia, Poland, Hungary, Germany and Austria in the vital formative period of their existence. Jews, too, introduced the element of messianism into youth movements claiming to be atheistic. That is as true of Marx and Trotsky as it is of Daniel Cohn-Bendit who, for all his hostility to his Jewish Christian heritage, is profoundly influenced by it.

But there is another constantly recurring phenomenon: what one might call the 'second exodus' – repudiation of the revolutionary parties and movements, leading very often and very swiftly to counter-revolutionary activities. It is not altogether surprising that orthodox party communists in both east and west should mistrust the Jews in their midst, for these Jews possess a very critical eye, both in regard to their parties and to themselves. The first effective critics of Lenin, and later of Stalin, were socialists and communists of Jewish extraction.

A frequent tendency of Jewish ex-communists – and one that is growing in significance today – is to return to the thought of their fathers and to revive respect for old and previously despised authorities.

This is the territory of the 'young conservative', whose importance – in Europe as well as in America – should not be underestimated. Since 1918 young conservatives have often helped (sometimes involuntarily) to open the door to the reactionaries. It was this coalition of reactionaries that brought Hitler to power in Germany, but one must also not overlook its pernicious influence in France, Italy and other European states in the years leading up to the Second World War.

Mao Tse-tung expressed his fear that the youth of China might stage a counter-revolutionary come-back. What conservative and reactionary politicians in the Soviet Union and the United States fear is that the young people in their countries might become revolutionary radicals. They are fully aware that these young people do not belong to them, though this does not stop them from being fully prepared to use their young generations as human material in their own defence.

In the next years and decades we can expect youth activity to proceed in a series of waves. There will be years of peace and quiet alternating with sudden, short-lived outbreaks of movement. The emergence of a youth internationale, comparable with the first and second internationales of the workers' movement, seems unlikely. It is true that, as youth increasingly takes on the status of a separate social class, the generation war will either supplant or at the least complement the class war. It is also true that, deep down, youth movements throughout the world are related to one another, and their ideas run parallel on many political, social and spiritual problems. But, on the other hand, the divergences of interest, the national distinctions, are stronger. To realise this, one has only to look at the young white people and the young black people of America. Added to that, there are always individuals and lone wolves – charismatic personalities who strut the stage for an hour as leaders, spokesmen and representatives of youth and precipitate a brief explosion. Two years later the political situation has changed, and three years later there is an entirely new generation entering the universities. Eighteen-year-old students cast uncomprehending eyes on twenty-five-year-olds who had once been revolutionaries – when they were twenty.

The pattern of the *Sturm und Drang* movement centred on the youth Goethe has been repeated by Mario Savio and his young Americans and by Kenichi Koyama and his *Zengakuren* in Japan: a swift rise and a sudden, unmistakable fall. But in the ashes fire still glows. Like the fabulous phoenix, young people throughout the ages have roamed the earth, seeking the fire that has eluded their fathers, in order to fashion a future which many of them will never live to see (sometimes, let it be said, to their own good fortune).

These young people adopt new fathers to lead them on the long march through the deserts of history into the promised land. All youth movements secretly worship at the shrine of a wandering god – a god of nomadic peoples, a moving volcano. It is their belief, sometimes cherished in secret, sometimes openly proclaimed in manifestos, that this volcano will consume all living idols and institutions. In a great act of creative destruction, it will smother all the old cities of Pompeii with its glowing lava. In this new and fruitful soil corn and vines, rice and laurels will grow, and on it will stand the cradle of the 'new man'. It was the dream of Shelley, of Byron and of Blake.

Thousands of years of disappointment and apparent failure have not succeeded in robbing our great youth movements of the will to pursue the great dream. And it is to their efforts of will that we owe all the successive stages of our civilisation.

Acknowledgments

Archiv für Kunst und Geschichte: 62.
Archiv Gerstenberg: 24, 25, 27, 37, 48L, 49, 78T, 102, 106T, 107, 108.
Associated Press Photo: 138, 168, 189.
Bildarchiv Foto Marburg: 19.
Bilderdienst Süddeutscher Vérlag: 58R, 64, 65, 66, 68B, 77B, 85, 88, 114, 119, 121, 171, 199.
Black Star: 127, 166, 211.
British Printing Corporation, 53.
F. Bruckmann Verlag, 7, 11.
Romano Cagnoni (Report): 124.
Camera Press: 141, 156, 212–3.
Galerie Delta, Berlin: 165.
Patrick Eagar (Report): 136.
John Freeman: 23.
John Hillelson Agency: 113, 142, 152, 160.
Historia, 44, 95.
Historical Institute, Amsterdam: 79.
Keystone Press Agency: 128, 129, 134, 188.
Mansell Collection: 8–9, 22, 28, 29B, 30–1, 33B, 40B, 41, 47, 54, 106B.
Mary Evans Picture Library: 29, 33T, 40T, 45, 82–3B.
Moro: 53.
Novosti Press Agency: 83T.
Photo Library, London: 112.
Hans Rachmann: 57, 58.
Radio Times Hulton Picture Library: 26, 43, 78B, 82T, 82B, 98–9, 118.
Staatsbibliothek, Berlin: 21.
Stern: 147, 174, 175, 177, 180–1, 182–3, 191, 202–3, 204.
Ullstein Bilderdienst: 67, 78–9, 90–1, 94, 104, 105, 109T.
Massimo Vitali (Report): 185.
Weidenfeld & Nicolson Archives: 109, 120T.
Wiener Library: 72.

Index

Abelard, Peter, 165
Abram, Morris b., 160
Adenauer, Konrad, 116, 120, 125, 172
Adorno, 177
Afghanistan, 139
Africa, 17, 81, 130, 134, 151, 200, 210
African states, 180
Albigenses, the, 16, 17, 144
Alcibiades, 10
Alexander the Great, 8
Alexander I, Tsar, 43, 78
Alexander II, Tsar, 86
Alexander III, Tsar, 86, 206
Algeria, 93
Allgemeine Deutsche Burschenschaft, 48
Altbach, Philip G., 150
America, 36, 52, 62, 80, 103, 129, 151, 210
  Central, 130; North, 200
  (see also United States);
  South, 21, 36, 130, 158, 190, 192, 193, 194, 195
American Anti-slavery Society, 145
American Civil War, 148
American War of Independence, 32
Amsterdam, 169
Arabian countries, 81, 130, 215
Arakcheyev, General, 78
Argentina, 21, 56
  Clouds, 10
Arnold of Brescia, 165
Arouet, Francoise-Marie, see Voltaire
Asia, 17, 137, 151, 200, 210
  discontented youth in, 215
Asia Minor, 15
Athenaeum, the, 45
Atkins, Robert, 158
Auschwitz, 67
Australia, 55
Austria, 55, 88, 93, 164, 215

Bachmann, 176
Baden-Powell, Lord Robert, 55, 56
  Scouting for Boys, 55
Baez, Joan 157
Bakunin, Mikhail, 79, 80, 87, 93, 136
Balkans, the, 51, 76, 79, 88, 100, 139
  the non-Islamic, 18
Barth, Karl, 61
Batista, 192
Baton Rouge university, 154
Beatles, the, 136, 158
beatniks, 133, 136, 137, 167
Becher, J.R., 67
Beethoven, Ludwig van, 26, 42
Belgium, 184
Belgrade, 94
Belinsky, 84
Berkeley, University of California in, 26, 145, 172, 186
  student unrest in, 155–60
Berlin, 63, 65, 72, 79, 101, 103, 116, 159, 164, 172, 176, 177, 186
  Berlin-Steglitz, 66; East, 172; Free University of, 172; Humboldt University, 72; West, 172, 173
betsdelnichestvo, 114
Bismarck, 63
Black Panthers, the, 154
Blake, William, 11, 23, 40, 41, 136, 218
  The French Revolution, 42; *Songs of Innocence*, 42
Blau-Weiss movement, 75
Bloch, Ernst, 20, 177
Bohemia, 18, 215
Bolshevists, the, 124, 177
Bosnia, 88, 93, 96, 100, 151
  West, 93
Bosnia-Hercegovina, 94, (see also Hercegovina)
Boy Scout movement, 55–7
  explorers, 56; raiders, 56; rover scouts, 56; wolf cubs, 56
Brandeis University, 160
Brazil, 20, 21

Brecht, 177
Britain, 39, 41, 65, 69, 80, 126, 127, 133, 139, 200
British American Biodynamic Association, the, 69
Brother Richard, 18
Brothers and Sisters of the Free Spirit, 16, 144
Brownsea Island, 55
Büchner, George, 153, 177
Budapest, 17
Bulgaria, 88
Bund deutscher Arbeiterjugend, 104
Bund deutscher Jugendvereine, 61
Bundestag resolution of 1835, 49, 50
Byron, Lord, 11, 23, 40, 42, 79, 218

Cabanyes, Manuel de, 51
Caesar, 8
Calcin, 20
California University, 136, 155, 160, (see also (Berkeley) Free University of, 157; Western University, 161
Calvinists, the, 21, 169
Camarra, Helder, 193
Camus, Albert, 35
Canada, 55, 148
capelloni, 133
Carbo, Juan Francisco, 51
Castro, Fidel, 136, 151, 195
Catalina, 10, 11
Catalonia, 79
Catholic Youth of Germany organisation, 61
The Challenge of Delinquency, 10
Charterhouse, 55
Chatterton, Thomas, 23
Chateaubriand, 34
Chema, see Saher, José Manuel
Chen Tu-hsin, 201
Chile, 55
China, 20, 21, 51, 111, 151, 197–206, 210
  last empress of, 200;

People's Republic of, 7, 130, 198, 200; revolutions, 200; Young, 201; youth risings, 197
Chinese Communist Party, 121, 202
Chinese Empire, 198
Chopin, 51
Christian church, 7, 17, 116
revival movements, 16, 17
Christian communism, 20, 184
Christianity, 15, 16
Christians, 148
early, 16, 69
Christlicher Verein Junger Männer, 60
Churchill, Sir Winston, 120, 122
CIA, 138, 164
Cicero, 8, 10
Civil rights movement, 123, 154
Clark, Dr Francis E., 60
CND, 170
Cohn-Bendit, Daniel, 37, 172, 179, 183, 184, 185, 186, 187, 216
Cohn-Bendit, Gabriel, 172, 186, 187
Coleridge, Samuel, 42
Collas, Count Carlo, 100
Columbia University, 159
Comités d'action lycéens (CALs), 178
Committee of Un-American Activities, 143
communist youth organisations, 111
Comsomol, 111, 112
Confucius, 179, 198
Constantinople, 101
Corbière, Tristan, 51
Cordoba Manifesto, 193, 194
Croatia, 18, 96
Crusaders, French, 17
Cuba, 51, 192
Curie, Madame, 89, 90
Cuvaj, Count, 96
Cvetko, Popović, 97
Czechoslavakia, 36, 120, 164

Dalmatia, 96, 97
Danton, 34, 35
Darrow, Clarence, 149
Decembrist rising, the, 78
Dedijer, Vladimir, 95
Delvig, 78
Desmoulins, Camille, 36,

37, 38
Djuka, 96
Dominican Republic, 192, 195
Dostoevsky, 80, 87
drugs, 50, 138, 139, 140, 144
Dutschke, Rudi, 62, 157, 175, 176

Eastern Orthodox Church, 76, 77, 93, 100
Eisenach, 52
Egypt, 15, 23, 215
Emerson, 138
Emindescu, 51
Encyclopaedia Britannica, 120
Endlicher, Ivan, 100
Engels, 177, 186, 206, 209
Enlightenment, English School of, 25
European, 78
Erasmus, 20
Erfurt Cathedral, 59
Erhard, Chancellor, 168, 172
Europe, 16, 18, 27, 34, 36, 39, 50, 51, 73, 78, 79, 81, 103, 129, 136, 164, 165, 167, 211; central and eastern, 18; western, 164, 200; young, 42, 45, 51
European Economic Community, 121
Evans, Sir Arthur, 93

Faban, 93
FBI, 138
Fenevitinov, 78
Feuer, Professor Lewis S., 159
First World War, 34, 55, 56, 61, 76, 101, 103, 105, 120, 194
Fischer, Karl, 66
Flower Power, 140, 143
Flusser, David, 15
Follen, Karl, 46, 52
France, 18, 23, 32, 34, 36, 40, 46, 51, 56, 69, 79, 126, 132, 149, 164, 195; revolts of 1830 and 1848, 88; student revolution in, 179-187
Franco regime, the, 21
Frankfurt, 65, 170, 176
Franciscans, the, 16, 17, 18, 93
Franz Ferdinand, Archduke, 76, 92, 95, 100

Franz Joseph, Emperor, 10, 91, 96
Free Speech Movement, 157
Freideutsche Jugend, 67, 68
French Revolution, the, 18, 32, 35, 36, 38, 39, 42, 44, 46
Freud, Sigmund, 177
Fries, J. F., 49

Garinovi, 93
Gammler movement, 133, 166-9
Gardiner, Rolf, 69
Gasperi, Alcide de, 120
Gaulle, General de, 179, 186
Geismar, 185
George III, King, 39
George IV, King, 43
German Democratic Republic, 67, 173, 177
German Federal Republic, 59, 60, 62, 73, 126, 130, 164, 173, 177
Germany, 21, 23, 24, 27, 32, 55, 58, 74, 88, 108, 116, 130, 139, 149, 151, 167, 178, 184, 215
East, 120; Empire of, 63; Hitler's, 115; romanticism in, 44-51; states of, 50; Young, 45, 49
Giessener Schwarzen, 46
Ginsberg, Allen, 137, 187
Sunflower Sutra, 137
girl guide movement, 56
Girondins, the, 35
Goeth, J., 23, 26, 27, 42, 46, 48, 218
The Sorrows of Young Werther, 23
Goldberg, Suzanne, 158
Gollwitzer, Professor Helmut, 67
Gorer, Geoffrey, 135
Göttingen, 25
Goya, Francisco, 51
Saturn Consuming his Sons, 51
Graeco-Roman civilisation, 10
Graubard, Stephen, 160
Greece, 43, 51, 130, 132, 167
Ancient, 7, 9; drama of, 10; Hellenistic period, 8
Greek independence war, 43

Grimm, Hans, 124
Volk ohne Raum, 124
Guardini, Romano, 59, 73
Schildgenossen, 59
Guatemala, 192
Guevara, Che, 7, 151, 177, 195
Gutzkow, Karl, 49

Habsburg family, 97, 100
Habsburg monarchy, 100
Hain, der, 24
Hamburg University, 174
Harlem, 159
Harrison, George, 136
Harvard, 52
Harvard University, 138, 148
Havana University, 194
Hegel, 34, 45, 75, 198
Heidegger, 75
Heimann, Eduard, 62
Heine, Heinrich, 46, 49, 184, 209, 216
Helwig, Werner, 59
Die Blaue Blume des Wandervogels, 59
Hercegovina, 88, 93
Herder, 25
Hermann, Professor G., 73
Herzel Theodore, 215
Hess, Rudolf, 67
Higginson, Thomas W., 149
hippies, 7, 16, 133, 138–144, 170, 209
Hitler, Adolf, 69, 74, 88, 92, 103, 105–10, 124, 164, 179, 215, 216, 217
Hitler-Jugend, 63, 72, 103–111, 115
Ho Chi Minh, 177
Hölderlin, Friedrich, 11, 34, 44, 45
Hölderlin, Karl, 44, 75
Holland, 50, 164, 184
Horkheimer, 177, 178
Huizinga, Jan, 169
Hungary, 18, 23, 50, 51, 52, 89, 120, 140, 164, 178

Ignatius de Loyola, 20, 21
Ilić, Todor, 100
India, 20, 21, 55, 151, 167, 215
intelligentsia, Russian, 80, 84
Iran, 139
Ireland, 116
Israel, 15, 75, 215, 216

Italy, 23, 50, 69, 79, 103, 156, 164, 184, 187
Young, 51

Jacobins, German, 46
Jacobs, Paul, 152
'The New Radicals', 152
Japan, 20, 80, 200, 207
Jefferson, Thomas, 161, 163
Jesuits, 21, 179
Jesus Christ, 15, 16, 17, 32, 42, 116, 197
Jimenez, Pérez, 192
Joan of Arc, 17
Johnson, President Lyndon, 141
Jordan, 93
Jukič, Luka, 96, 97
Jungstahlhelm, 104

Kamba, Professor Toshio, 209, 210
Kamba, Michiko, 209, 210
Kassof, Allen, 116
Keats, John, 23, 40, 42
Kenyatta, Jomo, 215
Kerensky, 86
Kerouac, Jack, 136, 137
The Dharma Bums, 137
Kerr, Clark, 155, 157, 160
Kinderkreuzzug, 178
King, Martin Luther, 154
Klatzer, Leo, 170
Klinger, Maximilian, 25
Sturm und Drang, 25
Kotzebue, 46, 52
Koyama, Kenichi, 218
Krasinski, 89
Kreisau, 69
Krupp, 64
Kruschev, 116, 209
Küchelbecker, 78
Kuffhäuser-jugend, 104
Kurella, A., 67

La Vista, 51
Labtsin, Alexander, 77
Lamberty, Muck, 59
Landau, Saul, 152
Larra, José, 50, 51
Latin America, (see America, South)
Laube, Heinrich, 49
Learmont, 79
Leary, Timothy, 138
Lemus, José, 192
Lenin, Vladimir Ulyanov, 10, 76, 84, 86, 87, 206
Lermontov, M. Y., 51, 79

'Prophecy', 79
Lerner, Michael, 158
Lima University, 192
Linne, Gerhard, 52
Lippman, Walter, 149
London, 41, 56, 133, 170, 177
London, Jack, 149
Luria, Salvador Edward, 161
Luria, Zelia, 161
Luther, Martin, 18, 19, 58, 178
Lutheranism, 18, 19, 21

Maistre, de Joseph, 77
Mameli, 51
Mao Tse-tung, 10, 108, 151, 177, 179, 198, 200, 203, 204, 205, 206, 209, 217
Marcuse, Herbert, 7, 34, 177
Marshall Plan, the, 121
Marx, Karl, 34, 45, 75, 80, 150, 157, 177, 184, 186, 198, 201, 206, 209, 216
May the Fourth Movement, 201, 202
Mayer, Fraulein, 40
Mazzini, 42, 51
Melanchthon, 18, 20, 128
Menzel, Herybert, 107
Merleau-Ponty, 75
Mexico, 56, 163, 190
Mickiewicz, 79, 87, 89
Konrad Wallenrod, 89, *Pan Tadeusz,* 89, *Dziady,* 89
Middle Ages, 16, 17, 123, 136, 188, 196, 205
Mills, Charles Wright, 150
Mississippi summer project, 145, 155, 157
Missolonghi, 43
Mo-Ti, 198
Moltke, Graf, 69
Montaigu, college of, 20
Montanists, the, 16
Moscow, 78, 84, 112, 209
Mundt, T., 49
Münzter, Thomas, 7, 19, 20, 177
Muravëv-Amursky, 80
Mussolini, 116, 187
Nadson, 85
Nanterre University, 129, 182, 183
Napoleon Bonaparte, Emperor, 18, 23, 34, 38, 44, 46

National Socialism, 60
National Socialist Party, 104, 106, 108, 111
National Socialists, 101, 115, 149
nationalism, European 18, messianic, 51
NATO, 121
Nature, worship of, 58
Nazis, 105
Neudeutschland, 60
New Left, the, 7, 20, 150
New Left Review, 150
New York, 138, 158, 159
  Free University of, 170
New Zealand, 55
nibonicho, 114
Nicholas I, Tsar, 79
Nicholas II, Tsar, 84, 206
Nietzsche, F., 32, 36, 68, 75, 97, 140, 201
Nievo, 51
Nixon, President Richard, 141
Nkrumah, Kwame, 215
Northern League, 78
Norway, 56
Novalis, 45, 75
Nyerere, Julius, 215

OAS, 187
Odoyevsky, Prince Vladimir, 78
Ohnesorg, Benno, 175
Orleans, 18
Ottawa, 56
Oxford, 149
Paine, Thomas, 42
Pakistan, 139
Palais Royal, 36
Pandurovi, Sima, 97
Pan-slavism, 87
Pappenheim, Martin, 101
Paraguay, 21
Paris, 17, 20, 35, 51, 65, 75, 79, 80, 172, 182
  student rising, 50, 132, 184–7; world exhibition, 111
Pascal, 36
Paul, Jean, 32
Peasants' revolts, 7
Peasants' War, 20
Peking, 112, 200, 209
Perez, Pablo Saher, 195
Pester Lloyd, 97
Petöfi, 51, 52, 89
Piferrer, Pablo, 51
Platter, Felix, 128
Poland, 18, 23, 32, 50, 51, 52, 88, 89, 120, 130, 140,

164; rebellions of 1830 and 1848, 88; freedom fighters, 89
'Polish October', the, 89
Portugal, 50, 116, 164
Potsdam, 106
Preporod, 92
Princeton, 148
Princip, Gavrilo, 93, 94, 95, 96, 97, 100, 101
Progressive Labour Party, 153
Prometheus, 25, 26, 42
Pross, Harry, 60, 63
Protestant church, 55
Protestantism, 58, 177
Provence, 17
provos, 7, 133, 166, 169–72
Prussia, 88
  East, 110
Pugachëv, 77
Purdue University, 135
Pushkin, 42, 78, 209
  Eugène Onegin, 42

Quickborn movement, 59, 60

Raitch, S., 78
Realschule, Linz, 92
Red Guards, 7, 198, 204, 205, (see also Young Guards)
Reich, Wilhelm, 7, 34, 177
Richter, Friedrich, see Paul, Jean
Rimbaud, 136, 167
  La Bohême, 167
Rio de Janeiro, 159
Rising of 1848, German, 52
Robespierre, 34, 35, 194
Roman Catholic Church, 15, 16, 55, 93, 100, 170, 192
Romans, the, 15
romanticism, English, 42; European, 42, 44; German, 78; political, 36
Rome, 18, 52, 123, 164, 176, 188, 189; ancient 7, 8, 10, 123
Roosevelt, Franklin D., 120, 122
R o s e n s t o c k - H u e s s y, Eugen, 62
Rosenzweig, Franz, 15
Rousseau, Jean-Jacques, 25, 32, 34, 35
  Du contrat social, 25
Rubin, Jerry, 143
Rudolf, Crown Prince, 10
Ruge, Arnold, 48, 184

Rumania, 69
Russia, 23, 32, 36, 40, 50, 51, 52, 88, 124, 139, 151, 200 (see also USSR)
  revolutionaries in the 19th century, 76–81
Rust, Franz, 67
Rydeyev, 78

Saher, José Manuel, 195
St Francis of Assissi, 17, 139
St Paul, 16
St Petersburg, 51, 79, 84, 86, 87, 88, 101
Saint-Just, Antoine de, 34, 35, 36, 37, 194
Saint-Simonists, 151
Sallust, 8
Salvador, 182
San Francisco, 137, 138, 156, 159
Sand, 46
Sarajevo, 92, 94, 95, 96, 97, 100
Sartre, J. P., 35, 75
Sauvageout, 185
Savio, Mario, 145, 156, 157, 158, 218
Schafft, Hermann, 61
  Neuwerk Jugend, 61
Schelling, 34, 45
Schiller, 26, 28, 32, 34, 177
  Die Räuber, 26, 27; Kabale und Liebe, 28; Rhenische Thalia, 32
Schirach, Baldur von, 106, 107, 108, 110, 116
Schlegel, 34, 45
Die Schönheit, 72
schools, 125–9; Adolf Hitler's, 110, 111; Balkan, 93, 96; English, 39; Polish, 90, 91
Schubart, 26
Schubert, Franz, 26
Schuman, Robert, 120
Schwarz-Rot-Gold, 104
Scipio Aemilianus, 8
SDS, 144, 173, 175
Second World War, 50, 62, 74, 93, 101, 116, 118, 130, 133, 164, 173, 187, 217
Seidmann, Peter, 122
Semis, José, 51
Senegal, 43
Serbia, 52, 94
Seume, J. G., 32

Shakespeare, William, 32
Shelley, Percy Bysshe, 11, 23, 39, 40, 42, 51, 218
    Defence of Poetry, 42;
    The Mask of Anarchy, 39;
    Prometheus Unbound, 42
Shih Hwang-ti, 198
Siberia, 78, 80
Siberski, Elias, 89
Sinclair, Upton, 149
The Sixteen, 79
Sklodowska, Marya, see Curie, Madame
Slovenia, 96
Slowacki, 89
Society for Devotees of Wisdom, 78
Society of Jesus, 20
Socrates, 10, 11
Soil Association, 69
    Mother Earth, 69
Somerville, Professor John, 161
Sophists, the, 10
Sorbonne, 185, 186, 187
South Africa, 55
Southern League, the, 78
Southern University, 154
Spain, 15, 21, 32, 50, 51, 116, 164, 184, 187
Spanish Civil War, 79, 149, 190
Spanish republic, 190
Spargo, John 149
Spender, Stephen, 40
Staël, Madame de, 34
Stagnelius, 51
Stalin, 80, 84, 87, 88, 116, 120, 195, 209
Stälin, Wilhelm, 61
Stanford University, 177
Steinberg, Jack, 157
stilyagi, 114, 115
Storzkowsky, 80
Streicher, Julius, 105
    Der Stürmer, 105
student movements, African, 214–5; American, 144–163; Chinese, 200–206, French, 179–87; Italian, 187–90; German, 172–9; Japanese, 207–211; Spanish, 190; South American, 192–5
Sturm und Drang movement, 218
Stuttgart, 28
Sulla, 10
Sun Yat-sen, 197, 200
Sweden, 50, 56, 139, 148

Switzerland, 55, 164
Syria, 15

teddy-boys, 114, 133
Terezin, 101
Third Reich, 111, 118
Thoreau, 138, 161, 163
    On the Duty of Civil Disobedience, 163
Thuringia, 28, 59
Tillich, Paul, 61
Tokyo, 159, 186, 209
Torres, Camilo, 193
Towianski, 51
Trotsky, 76, 84, 85, 86, 87, 136, 195, 216
Trujillo, Rafael, 192, 193
Tsinghua technical university, 204
Tübingen, 18
Tugendbund, 78
Turkey, 139
Turrisi-Colonna, 51

Ubico, Jorge, 192
Ukraine, the, 124
Ulbricht, 116, 121, 173
Ulyanov, Alexander, 85, 86, 87
Union Nationale des Étudiants Français, 187
Union of Soviet Socialist Republics, 112, 113, 114, 115, 116, 117, 120, 121, 130, 153, 173, (see also Russia)
United States of America, 21, 32, 34, 46, 52, 56, 62, 81, 89, 122, 126, 127, 130, 133, 134, 139, 172, 177, 178, 194, 200, 206, 217
students in, 144–166
United Nations, 122
Utagoe Undo, 209

Venezuela, 192, 195
Versailles, 24
Vidrič, Vladimir, 97
Vienna, 52, 88, 92, 101, 176
Vietnam, 21, 158
    North, 40
Voltaire, 34, 35
    La Loi Naturelle, 34
voyous, 133, 166
Vries, de, 169, 170

Waldenses, the, 16, 18, 144
Wanderbund, 75
Wandervogel movement, 58,

66, 72, 73, 74
    Der Wandervogel, 73
Warsaw Lyceum, 84, 90 186
Weber, Max, 173
Weimar Republic, 103, 108, 178
Welt, Theodore, 145
Werfel, Franz, 101
Wesilwski, 51
Wesley, John, 40
Wienbarg, L., 49
Wilhelm II, Kaiser, 63, 65
Wilson, E. B., 73
Wittenberg, 18, 19
Wordsworth, William, 42
World Alliance of Young Men's Christian Associations, 61
Wyneken, Gustav, 68

Yevtushenko, 116
yippies, 16, 137, 144, 209
Young Bosnians, 93, 95, 100
Young Guards, Mao's, 48, 108, 198
Young People's Society of Christian Endeavour, 61
Young Slovenes, 93
Young Socialists, 103
Youth, 201
Youth movements
    African, 48; Catholic, 59–62, 73, 116; Chinese, 203; Christian, 22, 55, 57, 59–62; European, 32; French, 34; German, 25, 34, 46, 48, 58, 63, 65, 68, 69, 72, 73, 75, 113, 178 215; Greek, 7–11; Protestant, 61–2, 73, 116; Russian, 76; Twentieth century, 139
Yugoslavia, 92

Zadar, 97
Zagreb, 96
Zen Buddhism, 137
Zengakuren, 208–10, 218
Zwingli, 128
Zürich, 159